ORGANIZATION DEVELOPMENT
A Practitioner's Tool Kit

Lenny T. Ralphs, Ph.D.

A FIFTY-MINUTE™ SERIES BOOK

CRISP PUBLICATIONS, INC.
Menlo Park, California

ORGANIZATION DEVELOPMENT
A Practitioner's Tool Kit

Lenny T. Ralphs, Ph. D.

CREDITS
Managing Editor: **Kathleen Barcos**
Editor: **Janis Paris**
Typesetting: **ExecuStaff**
Cover Design: **Carol Harris**
Artwork: **Ralph Mapson**

Distribution to the U.S. Trade:

National Book Network, Inc.
4720 Boston Way
Lanham, MD 20706
1-800-462-6420

Copyright © 1996 by Crisp Publications, Inc.

Printed in the United States of America by Bawden Printing Company.

Library of Congress Catalog Card Number 95-83114
Ralphs, Lenny T.
Organization Development
ISBN 1-56052-359-X

This book is printed on recyclable paper with soy ink.

LEARNING OBJECTIVES FOR:

ORGANIZATION DEVELOPMENT

The objectives for *Organization Development* are listed below. They have been developed to guide you, the reader, to the core issues covered in this book.

Objectives

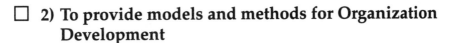

☐ 1) **To define and explain Organization Development**

☐ 2) **To provide models and methods for Organization Development**

☐ 3) **To discuss the role of the Organization Development consultant or change agent**

☐ 4) **To propose psychological strategies for managing change**

Assessing Your Progress

In addition to the Learning Objectives, *Organization Development* includes a unique new **assessment tool*** which can be found at the back of this book. A twenty-five item, multiple choice/true-false questionnaire allows the reader to evaluate his or her comprehension of the subject matter covered. An answer sheet, with a chart matching the questions to the listed objectives, is also provided.

* Assessments should not be used in any selection process.

TO THE READER

This book will be invaluable to anyone who wants to learn about Organization Development (OD) in a brief and simple format. In particular, this book was written for three main groups of readers.

1. *New Organization Development Consultants*—If you are a new OD consultant, this book is a simple reference manual to help you learn and remember many of the principles that are fundamental to this profession.

2. *Line Managers*—If you are a line manager who has to select and work closely with an OD consultant, or who is now required to do more OD work as an integral part of your daily role, this book is for you too.

3. *Experienced OD Practitioners*—Those of you who have been consultants in OD for some time will also find this a valuable tool and reference library. It will be helpful as a quick and simple way to review interventions and other OD practices. You can also use it as a simple way to help your clients become familiar with OD as you begin to work with them.

Lenny T. Ralphs

ABOUT THE AUTHOR

Lenny T. Ralphs has over 20 years of experience in Organizational Development and Training. He received His Masters in Organizational Behavior from BYU in 1974, and a doctorate in Organizational Communication from Kent State University in 1986. Early in his career, he was a manager of OD for a division of a Fortune 500 Company, with over 10,000 employees. In this capacity, he used the OD principles and practices from the boardroom to the plant floor.

Throughout his career, he has been instrumental in bringing about proactive change through OD principles and practices in every position he has held. He has been a corporate manager of training, a university faculty member, a vice president of a consulting force of more than 30, and is currently the vice president of seminar productions for Franklin Quest Co., a productivity training and consulting company.

ABOUT THE SERIES

With over 200 titles in print, the acclaimed Crisp 50-Minute™ series presents self-paced learning at its easiest and best. These comprehensive self-study books for business or personal use are filled with exercises, activities, assessments, and case studies that capture your interest and increase your understanding.

Other Crisp products, based on the 50-Minute books, are available in a variety of learning style formats for both individual and group study, including audio, video, CD-ROM, and computer-based training.

CONTENTS

CONTENTS (continued)

P A R T

I

Organization Development: An Overview

WHAT IS ORGANIZATION DEVELOPMENT?

Organization Development (OD) is a planned system-wide change using behavioral science and humanistic values, principles, and practices to achieve greater organizational performance and effectiveness. OD uses some form of diagnosis. OD is implemented by change agents who use a variety of interventions to achieve improved organizational health.

Let us look at each of these key words in the definition:

► **Planned Change.**   OD focuses on making changes that are planned in advance to achieve improvements.

► **System-Wide.**   The goal of the planned change is to improve the systems and processes in a part, or the whole, of the organization.

► **Behavioral Science.**   OD is based upon behavioral science assumptions and principles. These principles state that when people are open, trusting, mutually collaborative, and share common goals then greater individual group, and organizational effectiveness can be achieved.

► **Organizational Performance and Effectiveness.**   The organization is improved as a result of using the principles and practices of OD. The organization is healthier because of the planned change effort.

► **Diagnosis.**   Some method of diagnosis is used in all OD interventions to identify the scope and nature of the problem—be it surveys, interventions, observations, action research, or some other diagnostic technique.

► **Change Agent.**   Those who initiate the change effort are called change agents. Change agents use a number of interventions to achieve the planned change. The terms *change agent, consultant,* and *practitioner* will be used interchangeably in this book.

► **Interventions.**   The OD techniques used by change agents (or OD consultants) to achieve a planned change are called "interventions." These are the "tools" of the change agent.

HISTORY OF ORGANIZATION DEVELOPMENT

Organization development emerged from four major lines of theory and practice.

1. Laboratory Training
2. Survey Research
3. Action Research
4. Sociotechnical Systems Theory

Laboratory Training

In 1945 Kurt Lewin helped found the Research Center for Group Dynamics. Kurt Lewin had a strong background in group dynamics and influenced most of the individuals that went on to develop the theory and practice of OD. Lewin and his colleagues began to give feedback to group participants. This feedback and discussion of group processes later became known as "T-groups." These early works are the foundation for a great deal of "team building" and other group processes that we have today.

Survey Research

Survey research is the process of discovering the needs, feelings, and attitudes of employees within the organization. Once discovered, the information is analyzed and pulled together into a report that is "fed back" to management and employees. Any serious areas of employee concerns or attitudes become areas for OD problem solving and solutions.

Action Research

This is a collaborative effort with the client organization where researchers (or consultants) diagnose a problem. They then give feedback to the client of their findings and also deliver a plan for talking positive action. This on-going process of planning and taking action in collaboration with the client and consultant is "action reaseach."

Sociotechnical Systems Theory

The sociotechnical area of OD focuses on restructuring the work within the organization. We refer to this as "redesign" of work systems, "total quality," "self-directed work teams," and "reengineering."

OD PRINCIPLES

Not all of these principles apply in every OD situation, but some of them will be the underlying basis for every OD effort:

- Started at the top

- Dynamic and proactive

- Organic/Growth-oriented

- Interactive, using feedback loops

- Uses change agents

- Diagnostic and data oriented

- Experiential-learning based

- Focused on improved performance

- Strives for shared values

- Based on trust and empowerment

- Encourages open communication

- Moves toward participative style

- Emphasizes goal achievement

- Based upon behavioral sciences theory

- Adopts systems thinking

- Strives for improved effectiveness

- Action and survey research oriented

- Uses a practical approach to applied theory

- Works toward planned change

- Process oriented

- Balanced between people and performance

- Collaborative approach

EXERCISE

What values and principles are you most likely to adhere to in accomplishing an OD project?

_____

_____

_____

_____

_____

HOW DO YOU KNOW YOU NEED OD?

If you are a line manager or executive, you may be asking yourself, "How do I know if we need OD?" The answer: You know you need OD if your profits are down, your performance is down, the competition is passing you by, and your productivity is waning. Through working with your people, processes, and organizational systems, you can improve performance in individuals, teams and entire organizational systems using the technology of OD.

If you are experiencing any of the following in your organization then you most likely need OD. Place a checkmark in boxes that apply:

☐ Key individuals in the organization cannot get along and this is preventing the organization from performing at its peak levels or even endangering the very existence of the organization.

☐ People are unfocused and unclear about their personal and professional goals, which is causing wasted energy and ineffectiveness.

☐ Teams are performing poorly or ineffectively. The teams don't work together well because they don't understand their goals, roles and norms. They have poor problem-solving and decision-making skills, and don't know how to effectively share leadership and power. In general, they have weak and ineffective team processes resulting in poor performance.

☐ Teams are not only ineffective themselves, but they are also fighting with other departments or teams. Instead of focusing on the organization's shared mission and objectives, departments are wasting valuable time and effort on resource and turf battles that are entirely counterproductive and allow the competition to catch up or pass you by.

☐ Quality is poor, customer service is lousy, turnover is high, complaints are up, employee trust is low and so is morale—all signs that there are major problems in your systems and with your people.

☐ Your organization is out of touch with its clients, customers, and suppliers. The organization is out of touch with the external environments that impact the success or failure of the organization.

Overall, the systems, processes, and people are not working well and your organization is falling behind, ineffective, performing poorly or being passed up by the competition.

These are a few of the warning signs that may lead you to seek OD solutions to improving performance in the organization. Typically, every organization has these signs to one degree or another and will need to have an on-going OD effort to maximize the organization's competitiveness and performance.

Healthy/Unhealthy Organizations

Each of us as individuals has numerous systems working inside of us. Those systems are in varying states of health. When an individual is unhealthy, we see symptoms of poor health and take steps to correct the illness. Likewise the corporation or organization can be unhealthy, and we take steps to fix the situation. Taking steps to keep the organization as healthy and efficient as possible is the purpose of OD. Some of the characteristics of unhealthy and healthy organizations are given on pages 8–9.

The following points are adapted from the book *Managing With People*, by Jack Fordyce and Raymond Weil.

Characteristics of Unhealthy and Healthy Organizations

UNHEALTHY	HEALTHY
LEADERSHIP	
Top-down control of decisions	Decision making at all levels
Frequent bottlenecks	Organizational level not a factor
Manager is prescribing parent	Leadership is flexible and shifting
Control and justification	Freedom and trust
Excessive justifications required	High degree of autonomy
BUY-IN	
Nobody volunteers	Everyone pitches in
Nobody cares when things go wrong	Optimistic about problem solving
Mistakes and problems hidden	People signal awareness of problems
Only top-level investment in objectives	Objectives widely shared by all levels
Managers get minimum cooperation	Noticeable sense of team work
"It's *their* duty to save the ship."	"It's *my/our* responsibility to save the ship."
People feel locked in jobs	People involved by choice
Stale, bored, security-oriented	Excited, motivated, energized
PERSONAL/INTERPERSONAL	
Needs and feelings are side issues	Problem solving includes personal needs
Judgment at lower levels not respected	Judgment at lower levels is respected
Maskmanship and image building	Relationships are honest
People feel alone	People care about one another
Undercurrent of fear	Confidence and assurance

UNHEALTHY	HEALTHY
PROBLEM SOLVING	
Innovation in hands of a few	Everyone anticipates the future
Organizational charts dominate	Informal, nonterritorial
Pleasing management top priority	Boss is frequently challenged
Nonconformity frowned upon	Nonconformity encouraged
OFFICE POLITICS	
Conflict is covert	Conflict resolution is out in open
Office politics rampant	Not concerned with office politics
Policies and procedures hinder	Policies protect organizational health
Blame or withdrawal during crisis	People band together
Competition	Collaboration
Distrust of others' motives	Trust and acceptance
Help equals weakness	Help freely given and sought
PROGRESS	
One mistake and you are out	Willing to learn from each others' mistakes
Tradition!	High rate of innovation
Minimizing risk most important	Risk accepted as part of growth
Feedback is avoided	Feedback is growth
Learning is difficult	Learning is welcome and encouraged
Little or unhelpful feedback	Feedback sought, given and used

2

Organization Development Consultants

SELECTING OD CONSULTANTS

These are some of the questions you may want to ask as you select an OD consultant. If you are an OD external consultant, you may want to think about how you would answer these questions for your client.

Answer the following questions before you hire the consultant.

▶ *Why do you want to use an OD consultant?* _____

_____

▶ *Do you have a clear problem, opportunity, or purpose in mind?* _____

_____

▶ *What are your objectives?* _____

_____

▶ *What results do you expect?* _____

_____

▶ *What do you expect the OD consultant to do?* _____

_____

▶ *What level of expertise do you expect the OD consultant to have?* _____

_____

▶ *Do you need a specialist or a generalist in OD?* _____

_____

▶ *What responsibilities do you expect the consultant to assume?* _____

_____

▶ *What responsibilities do you expect the client organization carry out?* _____

_____

▶ *What is your budget?* _____

_____

SELECTING OD CONSULTANTS (continued)

► *What return do you expect for your investment?* _____

_____

► *How will you measure/evaluate success of the work?* _____

_____

Questions to Ask References

Clearly, you will want to check some references. Here are some key questions to ask when you speak to the references? Place a checkmark in the boxes after you have asked each question.

☐ How long have you known the consultant?

☐ How did you get to know them?

☐ How effective were they in the work they did for you?

☐ Why would you recommend them for our work?

☐ Were they easy to work with?

☐ Were they effective and productive?

☐ What did they charge?

☐ Were there any contract problems?

☐ Were they successful?

☐ Would you hire them again?

You may want to follow each of the above questions with a "why or why not" question in order to probe deeper to arrive at more comprehensive information.

Following are some questions you could ask the OD consultant.

► *How long have you been doing this?* _____
_____

► *Tell us about the work you have done in the past.* _____
_____

► *What are the greatest successes you have had in this work and why?* _____
_____

► *What were your greatest failures and why?* _____
_____

► *What are your basic consulting values, beliefs, and assumptions you use in this work?* _____
_____

► *How would you describe your personal style in this work?* _____
_____

► *How can we tell if you are competent?* _____
_____

► *How do we know we can trust you?* _____
_____

► *What do you charge?* _____
_____

► *When could you start?* _____
_____

SELECTING OD CONSULTANTS (continued)

▶ *What would you describe as the overall process and schedule?* _____
_____

▶ *What would be your first three steps?* _____
_____

▶ *How can we measure your success? Our success?* _____
_____

▶ *Are there any other questions we should ask you at this point?* _____
_____

▶ *Do you have any additional questions of us?* _____
_____

This method is NOT recommended!

OD VALUES

In a survey of some 1,000 OD practitioners, Van Eynde and associates asked three key questions of the practitioners regarding their OD values and what attracted them to the field of OD. How would you answer these questions? Compare your answers to those given by those from the survey:

Question #1 What attracted you to OD?

_____

_____

_____

Overall, respondents said they were attracted by a desire to:

✔ Create a change

✔ Have a positive effect on people and organizations

✔ Enhance the effectiveness and profitability of organizations

✔ Learn and grow

✔ Exercise power and influence

Question #2 What values are associated with OD work today?

_____

_____

_____

The values fell into two major categories—"performance" and "process." Performance values have to do with effectiveness and productivity. Process values have to do with empowerment, open communication, and participation. The trend is moving toward process values.

OD VALUES (continued)

> **Question #3 What values should be associated with future OD work?**

_____

_____

_____

The five values that respondents rated highest or most important to future OD practitioners are as follows:

- ✔ Empowering employees

- ✔ Creating open communication

- ✔ Promoting a culture of collaboration

- ✔ Promoting inquiry and continuous learning

- ✔ Facilitating the ownership of process and outcome

All five relate to organizational processes. Values related to organizational outcomes—such as effectiveness, productivity, and profitability—were rated lower, or as less important.

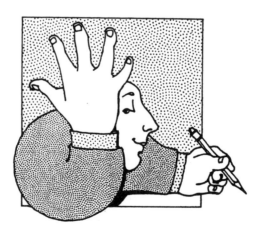

OD COMPETENCIES

There are four areas of effectiveness—practitioner skill areas, competency categories, practitioner behaviors, and intervention outcomes—that are key to OD competency (Eubanks, Marshall and Driscoll, 1990).

Practitioner Skill Areas

- People skills
- Data skills
- Delivery skills

Competency Categories

- Using interpersonal skills
- Managing group processes
- Using data

- Contracting
- Implementing the intervention
- Maintaining the client relationship

Practitioner Behaviors

- Gain management support
- Collaborate
- Prepare
- Adapt to change
- Establish rapport
- Facilitate group processes

- Demonstrate professionalism
- Use client's language
- Resolve client issues
- Establish explicit contract
- Collect data
- Follow up

OD COMPETENCIES (continued)

Intervention Outcomes

The intervention outcomes include four primary areas of assessment:

1. GOAL SETTING

Here the research team assessed the items that showed the extent to which practitioners and their clients:

- Felt that program goals were specific, measurable, and time-bound
- Felt that goals were set by the practitioner, management, or in collaboration with all organization stakeholders

2. INTERVENTION ACTIVITIES

The team also assessed whether the processes designed by the practitioner had the following characteristics:

- Were flexible or responsive to the needs of the organization
- Involved support from top management within the organization
- Involved collaboration with the organization in designing the program
- Helped make rewards contingent on performance
- Helped move power and communication to the people who do the work
- Helped move knowledge downward through the organization
- Established the organization's ownership of the change process

3. INTERVENTION RESULTS

The results of a practitioner change program were assessed by asking respondents to indicate the extent to which the program accomplished the following objectives:

- Increased knowledge about organizational effectiveness
- Increased profits
- Increased satisfaction with the organization
- Yielded higher performance by the work groups for whom the program was targeted
- Produced better leadership and management skills
- Improved group functioning
- Increased the ability of individuals to attain personal goals

4. ORGANIZATIONAL OUTCOMES

This item indicated the extent to which the practitioner program met the following criteria:

- Was worth the cost in both money and time
- Was effective
- Was acceptable to all involved
- Presented no disadvantages to others
- Was at the right depth for the situation

Organization Development Skills Checklist

Below is a partial list of core skills that future OD practitioners will need. Review the list now and place a checkmark in boxes by those skills that you now possess. For all the skills that you still need to develop, begin to form an action plan to start acquiring the skills that will keep you competitive.

☐ Organizational diagnosis	☐ Questionnaire design
☐ Design and execute interventions	☐ Writing proposals and reports
☐ Interviewing and observation	☐ Rational-emotive skills
☐ Conceptual and analytical ability	☐ Group dynamics
☐ Organizational theory/design	☐ Leadership and power
☐ Conflict management	☐ Motivation
☐ Large system change theory	☐ Job design
☐ Active listening	☐ Giving and receiving feedback
☐ Coaching and counseling	☐ Data analysis
☐ Public speaking and training	☐ Management savvy and strategy
☐ Process consultation	☐ Action research
☐ Credible behavorial modeling	☐ Build trust and rapport

OD CONSULTANT'S ROLE

What role does the OD consultant perform in the OD process? The OD consultant differs from the typical technical consultant because OD technology does not limit itself to solving problems within any one particular area such as marketing, engineering, finance, or MIS. Instead, OD consultants solve problems in processes, systems, teams, individuals, organizational cultures, structures, and designs within every area in the organization. The role focuses on improving organizational performance and effectiveness through diagnosis and interventions.

The following are some of the actions that are typical roles the OD consultant performs in the client's organization to bring about positive change:

- ► Confronting old ways

- ► Helping people get out of comfort zones

- ► Helping to achieve an open and trusting environment

- ► Providing insights on how to stay on track toward the new vision

- ► Providing expertise in teambuilding, systems redesign, and other behavioral science interventions

- ► Balancing the power in groups and organizations

- ► Questioning the "traditional " or "bureaucratic" practices

- ► Facilitating different views and perspectives

- ► Helping to minimize conflicts over "territory"

- ► Helping to move toward "high performance" teams and systems

- ► Helping to achieve a "healthy" organization

- ► Helping to adapt productively to change

- ► Assisting to close the gap between the current state and the positive future state

EXTERNAL VERSUS INTERNAL CONSULTANTS

An internal consultant is someone who is working inside the organization and is on the organization's payroll as an employee. The external consultant is neither on the payroll nor a fulltime employee of the organization. Here are some of the typical strengths or advantages for each kind of consultant.

ADVANTAGES OF EXTERNAL CONSULTANT

- Has outside objectivity and point of view

- Has fewer organizational biases

- Has more power

- Has greater freedom

- Is more experienced with organizations

- Is assigned more authority and "expert status"

- Can risk more

- Can confront more

ADVANTAGES OF INTERNAL CONSULTANT

- Is more familiar with the organization's norms and culture

- Knows the organization's technology better

- Understands the communication networks and politics

- Has minimal or no "outsider" stigma

- Is more loyal to the organization's long-term success and health

Working As a Team

Most consultants agree that for the best results the internal and external OD consultants should work together as a team. Usually the disadvantages of one are the advantages of the other and visa versa. So working together they have the advantages of both.

OD CONSULTANT STYLES

The following are four consulting styles. They may not be mutually exclusive. Which of them would you consider to be most like your style in general?

STYLE	EMPHASIS IS ON:	LANGUAGE:
Diagnoser	Diagnosis and analysis	"Let's diagnose before we go too far so we don't go down the wrong path."
Doer	Immediate action	"Let's dig in and solve this problem as we go. We'll learn to do by doing."
Director	Authority and expertise	"I've learned from experience, so I'll give them clear direction on what needs to be done."
Developer	Building trust and openness	"I'll develop their trust so we can effectively solve the problems together."

Which Style is Most Like You?

Diagnoser	**Doer**
Director	**Developer**

What is your consulting style? One of the most important things you will do as a consultant is to clearly think through what you stand for and what approach or style you will practice. There probably isn't one style that fits everyone nor a style that is the only right way in every situation, but there is a style that is more like you and fits the way you like to work in most situations.

EXERCISE

Think through and jot down the answer to these questions for yourself:

1. How would you describe the ideal consultant style?

   _____

   _____

   _____

   _____

2. Is this ideal style your style today? If not, what do you need to do to achieve this ideal style?

   _____

   _____

   _____

   _____

3. Will this ideal style be effective in every client relationship? Why or why not?

   _____

   _____

   _____

   _____

DEVELOPING TRUST

A key to success in consultant-client relationships is the development of trust in the relationship. Following are some of the characteristics that are a part of successfully developing trust:

Authenticity

The consultant is not fake. There is no gamesmanship. What you see is what you get.

Congruency

The consultant is consistent. Words match behaviors.

Openness/Honesty

You know when you communicate with them that they will always respond in an open and honest manner.

Fairness/Objectivity

They are fair and objective in their judgments. They minimize their biases.

Reflection/Empathy

They listen well and accurately reflect back not just what you are saying, but the feeling behind your words. They are empathetic and understanding.

Self-Disclosing

They are secure enough about themselves that they can talk openly about themselves, their values, beliefs, and assumptions. They are not afraid to admit failure or claim successes, putting them into a healthy perspective.

Competency

They have enough confidence and expertise in their work to know they are competent. Because of their competence, you feel comfortable trusting their advice and direction.

THE CONTRACT MEETING

Here are some of the things that need to be done in the contract process. There will almost always be a contract meeting where the consultant and client will iron out details of both a written and psychological contract. Some things will be agreed upon prior to the meeting, but most will be done at the meeting.

Preliminary to Meeting (face-to-face or by phone)

- What's the general need/problem/opportunity facing the organization? _____

  _____

- Who in the organization wants this done and why? _____

  _____

- How soon do you want to begin? _____

If you choose to go further, you will decide the following:

- When could we meet? _____

- Who will be at the meeting? _____

- What do we expect to accomplish at this initial meeting? _____

  _____

The Meeting

The contract meeting(s) is where the consultant and the client work out the contract for the project/process. In some cases, the agreement may be simple enough that both parties just agree informally and verbally. In other cases the contracting may be more formal and include simple to complex written contracts. The key to successful contracting is to overcommunicate and clarify as much as possible at the onset. The following is a contract list that outlines many of the key questions that need to be addressed during contracting with the client. Blank lines are provided at the end of each area for you to write some of your own questions that may not have been addressed here:

CONTRACT CHECKLIST

Expected Results/Outcomes:

► What are the client's objectives? _____

► What results do they expect to accomplish? _____

► What outcomes would they like to see? _____

► Can you (the consultant) deliver these results/expectations? _____

► What are the client's expectations? _____

Additional questions:

_____

_____

Resources and Time:

► How much is the client willing to spend in terms of money and resources to accomplish the objectives? _____

► What are the consultant's fees and pay schedule? _____

► How long will this take? _____

► When do we get started? _____

► Overall what will take place in terms of diagnosis? Interventions? Other?

_____

_____

► Who will be involved from the client organization and for how much time? _____

_____

► Who will be the contact point? _____

_____

Additional questions:

_____

_____

Roles:

► What roles will the client perform? _____

► What roles will the consultant perform? _____

► What roles will we mutually perform? _____

Additional questions:

_____

_____

Ground Rules:

► What are the ground rules? _____

► Confidentiality? _____

► Openness and trust? _____

► Meetings, agendas and so on? _____

► Responsibilities? _____

► Follow-through? _____

_____

Additional questions:

_____

_____

Other:

► How will we evaluate our progress? _____

► Can either party renegotiate the contract if things are not working out? _____

_____

Additional questions:

_____

_____

WARNING SIGNS: SOMETHING HAS GONE WRONG

There are times when the consultant may run into trouble in the consulting process. Be aware of these warning signals:

1. Confidentiality is broken.

2. The timing is just not right. It is too much of an emotionally charged situation for now, so you have to back off for a time.

3. The client, for their own ends, tries to manipulate you into harming or threatening an individual or group.

4. The promises for resources and time agreed to in the initial contract are falling short.

5. The support of top management and key players is just not there.

If Something Goes Wrong Ground Rule

Chris Argyris, a well-known author and consultant, has a ground rule he calls the "one minute or one hour" rule. It is simply this. If things are not going as expected, either party can pull out of the project at anytime on a "minute's notice" but they must be willing to spend "an hour" discussing the decision to pull out.

P A R T

3

Diagnosis

WHAT IS DIAGNOSIS?

The doctor-patient relationship is similar to OD. The practitioner must do some kind of diagnosis to determine what needs to be done before a prescription can be given. Unlike the doctor-patient relationship, the OD consultant will typically be more interactive with the client. In the OD process it is frequently the case that the client works hand-in-hand with the consultant to solve the problem. The values of an OD approach encompass a high degree of "ownership" and "mutual collaboration" with the client throughout the process including the diagnostic phase.

The purpose of a diagnosis is to identify the problem or opportunity in order to correct the problem or capitalize on the opportunity. The process includes some kind of data collection, analysis of the data, and feedback of the data to the client.

Diagnostic Process Flow

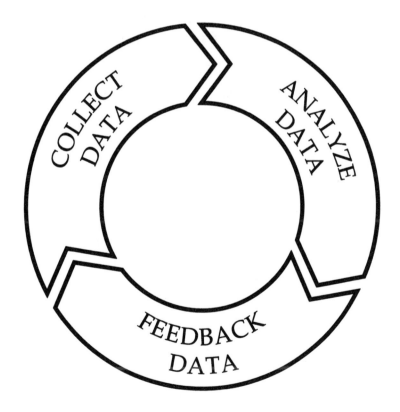

GAP ANALYSIS

Another way of looking at diagnosis is a "gap analysis." As a practitioner you identify with the client the ideal standard of performance they would like to achieve. Once you have mutually identified where you would like to be ideally, then you can identify where the client is now in relationship to the standard. The difference between where you are now and where you want to be is the "gap" that needs to be addressed.

Gap Analysis

The extent to which the OD practitioner can accurately help the client diagnose the performance gaps and close them is the nature of success in the OD process.

DIAGNOSTIC TRUST BUILDING

In the beginning of the diagnosis you will typically have some critical issues that you need to address. The people in the client system that you have to get the data from will often have some degree of distrust or resistance. They may be afraid this diagnosis will lead to change that they cannot live with. Or, they think they may lose something if things change. There are a number of questions they may have on their minds that you will have to answer for them in order to build enough trust to get accurate data. Here are some of those questions:

⚷ 12 KEY QUESTIONS

1. Who are you?

2. What are you doing here?

3. Why are you doing this?

4. How do I know I can trust you?

5. What will happen to the information I give you?

6. Why should I tell you the truth?

7. How do I know you will keep a confidence?

8. Who exactly will see this information/report?

9. Will I be mentioned by name or recognized in any way?

10. How do I know anything worthwhile will happen as a result of this?

11. Will I get some feedback on the results of this diagnosis, and when will it occur?

12. Are you really going to deliver on what you have promised?

DIAGNOSTIC MODELS

Practitioners use a number of tools to accomplish their work. These tools fall into two major categories—*models* and *interventions.* We will talk about interventions in some detail in the last section, but now let's talk about two key models of OD. These models provide a framework for the practitioner to view the organization or situation. This framework helps the consultant work through the issues in an organized way to come up with solutions. Without good models it would be easy to get off track, lose focus, or become totally ineffective in the OD effort.

An Action Research Model for OD

In OD we learn more about the client in every stage of the process. While diagnosis may be primarily done in the beginning of the OD process, it is usually ongoing. The OD process is an interactive research process where data is collected, analyzed, and fed back. Action is taken on what is learned and the cycle is repeated. This process is called an "action research model." This model is one of the most widely known models in OD practice. Not only is it a diagnostic model, but it is also a problem-solving process.

Action Research Model

etc.

Joint action planning (Objectives of OD program and means of attaining goals, e.g., "team building")

Feedback to key client or client group

Further data gathering

Data gathering and diagnosis by consultant

Consultation with behavioral scientist consultant

Key executive perception of problems

Action (new behavior)

Action planning (determination of objectives and how to get there)

Discussion and work on data feedback and data by client group (new attitudes, new perspectives emerge)

Feedback to client group (e.g., in team-building sessions, summary feedback by consultant; elaboration by group)

Data gathering

Action

Action planning

Discussion and work on feedback and emerging data

Feedback

Data gathering (reassessment of state of the system)

SOURCE: Copyright 1969 by the Regents of the University of California. Reprinted from *California Management Review,* Vol. XII, No. 2, p. 26, Figure 1. By permission of the Regents.

The Force Field Analysis Model

In addition to the action research model just mentioned, the force field analysis model is probably the most widely known model in OD. Kurt Lewin, one of the early pioneers of OD, is given credit for it.

Force Field Analysis

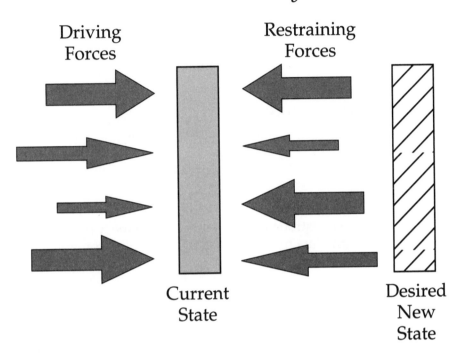

Driving Forces   Restraining Forces

Current State   Desired New State

The model proposes two types of forces keeping any system frozen in a state of equilibrium. The arrows on the left represent the forces for change or the "driving" forces, and the arrows on the right represent the forces maintaining the status quo or the "restraining" forces. The area in the middle represents the status quo or the current level of performance. The length or width of an arrow represents its relative strength, with the longer and wider lines being the strongest. The vertical or parallel line on the right represents the desired new level or state that the individual or organization wants to move toward.

Used as a diagnostic model the consultant would use interviews, surveys, and other such data collection techniques to find out what people believe to be the forces for and against change in the organization as well as the relative strength of these forces. At a later meeting (to feed back the data and work toward the solution) the group that shared the data in the first place will usually have an opportunity to suggest ways to eliminate or weaken the restraining forces—or strengthen or add to the driving forces so the new state can be achieved. The goal is to "unfreeze" the status quo and move to a new level and then "refreeze" at the new level or state.

PROBLEMS IN DIAGNOSIS

There are several problems a practitioner may run into as they conduct the diagnosis. Some of the more common ones can occur in the following areas.

► **CLIENT TRUST**

People have a difficult time trusting someone who is seeking to change the organization. Even when some of the clients trust the practitioner, others may not. It is a constant battle to build trust and rapport quickly enough an deeply enough to obtain meaningful data.

► **CLIENT PARTICIPATION**

They don't want to be a part of the process. Not all, but some will resist by trying to avoid the process altogether.

► **CLIENT BIAS**

Some may have very strong biases that will get in the way. Even if they give the consultant data freely and willingly it may be contaminated because of their biases.

► **CONSULTANT BIAS**

You probably have your own set of biases. How do you work through your own biases as a consultant in order to maintain objective judgments?

► **DATA-HANDLING BIAS**

You could have too much or too little data from one source or area, thus causing bias in the sample. How do you balance this in order to avoid this type of bias?

► **TOP MANAGEMENT OPENNESS**

Once the data is collected and fed back to management, they may not want to share the data with others because it is too negative or sensitive. In some cases they may want to be punitive because their egos are bruised.

► **JUMP TO CAUSE**

We "jump to cause" just as we would jump to conclusions. We see symptoms early on and immediately assume we know what caused the problem.

DATA COLLECTION METHODS

There are five commonly used types of data-gathering methods (Burke, Clark, and Cooper, 1984).

1.	One-on-one interviews	87%
2.	Observations	60%
3.	Group interviews	52%
4.	Questionnaires	45%
5.	Documents	37%

Typically, practitioners use a variety of methods rather than relying on only one.

A Comparison of Different Methods of Data Collection

Method	Major Advantages	Major Potential Problems
Interviews (Individual and Group)	1. Adaptive—allows data collection on a range of possible subjects 2. Source of "rich" data 3. Empathic 4. Process of interviewing can build rapport	1. Expense 2. Bias in interviewer responses 3. Coding and interpretation data 4. Self-report bias
Observations	1. Collects data on behavior, rather than reports of behavior 2. Real time, not retrospective 3. Adaptive	1. Coding and interpretation difficulties 2. Sampling inconsistencies 3. Observer bias and questionable reliability 4. Expense
Questionnaires	1. Responses can be quantified and easily summarized 2. Easy to use with large samples 3. Relatively inexpensive 4. Can obtain large volume of data	1. Nonempathy 2. Predetermined questions/missing issues 3. Overinterpretation of data 4. Response bias
Unobtrusive measures (Documents and reports)	1. Nonreactive—no response bias 2. High face validity 3. Easily quantified	1. Access and retrieval difficulties 2. Validity concerns 3. Coding and interpretation difficulties

SOURCE: D. Nadler, *Feedback and Organization Development: Using Data-Based Methods*, © 1977 by Addison-Wesley Publishing Co. Reprinted by permission of Addison-Wesley Publishing Co., Inc. Reading Mass., p. 119.

SURVEY FEEDBACK

Survey feedback usually involves a variety of data collection techniques, most commonly the questionnaire. Survey feedback is a form of action research. It is both a diagnostic tool and an intervention. As the name implies, *survey feedback* includes a survey of some type. The survey is usually given to the entire client organization. The questionnaire is designed to find out about or diagnose several key areas of organizational health such as leadership, decision making, manager-employee relations, empowerment, and overall satisfaction in a number of areas.

As the name also implies, after the survey is administered and analyzed, the results of the survey are fed back to the people in the organization. There is an implied, if not actual, contract with people who are surveyed that they will get back a summary of the results of the data they gave when they filled out the survey. The data is anonymous when the survey results are given back. Usually, this feedback is given at a feedback meeting.

Feedback Meetings

After data is collected and analyzed, it must be fed back to those that gave the data in the first place. The most common way of doing this is a face-to-face meeting. The purpose of the meeting is to:

- Develop ownership

- Give back results

- Increase motivation to keep the process going

- Fulfill the promises made in collecting the data

- Get a sense of the pockets of resistance and acceptance

- Lay the groundwork for the next step such as interventions, planned change, and so on.

Some of the feedback meetings are large and include the entire client system. Others are small, with only a few members at a time in order to allow for maximum opportunity for questions and interaction. Some meetings are as short as an hour or two, and some take several days and include an immediate problem-solving intervention addressing the data.

P A R T

4

Planned Change

WHAT IS PLANNED CHANGE?

As discussed earlier, during the diagnostic phase of the OD process a gap is identified between where the organization is currently and where it would like to be. At that point we want to close the gap. To do that we have to change. Like any other discipline or technology, to change will require some type of planning. This is where the notion of planned change is derived.

Planned change is accomplished through the OD interventions. We will discuss interventions in some detail in the next section. These interventions serve to change the behaviors of individuals, groups, or entire organizations. There is a range of change, focusing from overcoming resistance to creating a proactive vision for future change.

The following five-step model contributes to the effective management of change.

A Five-Step Change Management Model

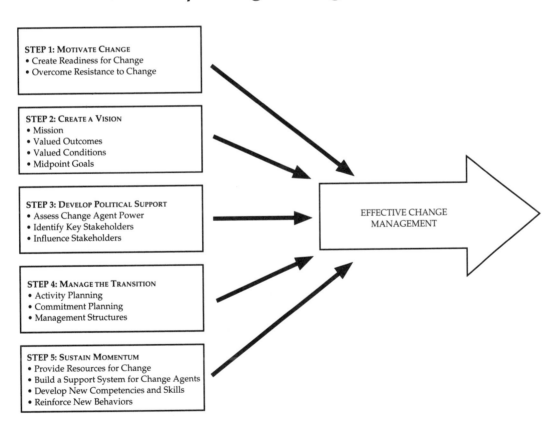

STEP 1: MOTIVATE CHANGE
• Create Readiness for Change
• Overcome Resistance to Change

STEP 2: CREATE A VISION
• Mission
• Valued Outcomes
• Valued Conditions
• Midpoint Goals

STEP 3: DEVELOP POLITICAL SUPPORT
• Assess Change Agent Power
• Identify Key Stakeholders
• Influence Stakeholders

STEP 4: MANAGE THE TRANSITION
• Activity Planning
• Commitment Planning
• Management Structures

STEP 5: SUSTAIN MOMENTUM
• Provide Resources for Change
• Build a Support System for Change Agents
• Develop New Competencies and Skills
• Reinforce New Behaviors

EFFECTIVE CHANGE MANAGEMENT

Adapted from Cummings and Worley *Organization Development and Change.* St. Paul, MN: West Publishing, 1993. (With permission of the publisher.)

STAGES OF CHANGE: THE FOUR A'S

There are four basic stages that people experience when they go through a change process:

Ambivalence: The person in this stage experiences shock, disbelief, and fear.

Anger/**A**pathy: This is the "fight or flight" stage. At this stage the person experiences anger and/or depression or both. They resist the change either overtly or covertly. Or, they may just pretend it doesn't exist and hope it will go away.

Adjustment: At this stage they begin to adjust to the new state or reality. They stop fighting it and start figuring out how to live with it. They may test out new behaviors and see what is going to work.

Acceptance: At this stage they have accepted the new reality or change state and have adopted new behaviors that are in harmony with the new status quo.

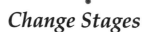

Change Stages

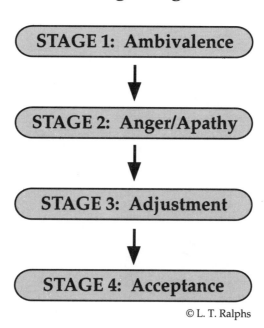

© L. T. Ralphs

REASONS PEOPLE RESIST CHANGE

"It is difficult to expect people who are fearful to accept a whole lot of change." In a study by Smye and Cooke of organizations who failed to shift gears successfully during the change effort, the researchers found the following:

- In 40 percent of the cases, the firms failed because they lacked the capability to execute the strategy.

- In 35 percent of the cases, the firms failed because the organization was not "change ready" or committed.

- Only 17 percent of the failures were attributed to poor strategy.

According to the study's authors, "There is a very human answer to why strategies derail. They depend on people for successful execution, and massive change creates fear in most people. Fear is inherently human and is the enemy of change. To achieve change, we must first conquer people's fear of it."

This approach is guaranteed to fail!

THE TEN GREATEST "FEARS OF CHANGE"

FEAR #1   Loss of Job

In 1992 and 1993 alone, large organizations like IBM, AT&T, and GM laid off over 600,000 people.

FEAR #2   Loss of Pay

One of the largest budget areas is salaries. Organizational change may result in one's pay being cut in the current job or having to take a job that pays less.

FEAR #3   Loss of Status

In some cases a change will bring about a demotion—or, the responsibilities change and you lose status and other privileges.

FEAR #4   Loss of Friends

When change occurs we sometimes lose the positive relationships we enjoyed with peers or others in the organization.

FEAR #5   Loss of Benefits

In some situations when change occurs the benefits we had are no longer as good. We have less time off, less health coverage, fewer personal leave days, and so forth.

FEAR #6   Loss of Physical Comfort Zones

We may have to change our office or work location. We may have to travel more to places we don't care to go to. We may have to change our schedule of hours or days worked.

FEAR #7   Feelings of Incompetence or Obsolescence

We fear that our skills and knowledge will become outdated, that we cannot keep up, or that some form of technology will replace us.

FEAR #8   Working Harder

We are afraid that when someone goes away, such as in layoffs, those of us that remain will have to work harder to keep up.

FEAR #9   Personal Loss

We fear that the change will cause us to work more hours and have less time for family or leisure than we had before.

FEAR #10   Communication Loss or Overload

We may no longer be a part of the networks that keep us in the "know." Or, we may have too much information coming to us through electronic mail, voice mail, direct mail, reports, news and so on.

OTHER REASONS WE RESIST CHANGE

All of us have had instances where we resisted change. Place a check in the boxes that identify a reaction you have had in the past.

☐ "I don't know how to change." In some cases we may want to change but we don't know how to change.

☐ "It's not my problem." We believe we didn't create the problem so we shouldn't have to solve it. Just let someone else fix it.

☐ "What's in it for me?" No payoff. Either we perceive there will be a reward or we will be able to avoid some pain.

☐ "It doesn't fit my values." We believe this change will go against our cores values and beliefs.

☐ "It wasn't my decision." No ownership. We resist most changes where we have little or no involvement in the decision to change.

☐ "I don't like the 'changer.'" We resist the change because we don't like or trust the person(s) asking us to make the change.

☐ "I don't like the means." We sometimes are not resisting the change itself but "how" it is being done. If we perceive someone is manipulative or condescending we may resist even if we agree with the change.

☐ "It's a passing fad." If we perceive this to be a whim or passing fad we will not want to put forth the effort to support it.

☐ "I don't want the responsibility." In any change there is a degree of responsibility that must be accepted to achieve the change. Some people just don't want to accept the responsibility involved.

☐ "There is a lack of direction or no clear goals." If we are unclear of the direction or goal, we may hold back or be unable to proceed.

☐ "It has always been done this way so why change it?" Tradition! Traditions run long and deep and sometimes it is difficult to change the tried and true even if the ship is sinking.

When the need is great enough we will overcome any fear of change or any other reason for resistance to change. The skillful change agent uses a variety of tools to facilitate overcoming these barriers to change and bringing about acceptance of change for healthy growth and renewal.

WHY PEOPLE ACCEPT CHANGE

Change is neither bad or good. It is often a matter of how we look at it. Some people perceive all change to be bad. Others see most if not all change to be good.

In those situations where change happens and we have absolutely no control over it, we still have a choice—we can always choose our *reaction* to the change. We can choose to be proactive or reactive, to fight or flight, to become despondent or be optimistic, to resist or accept. Those that seem to handle change in the most productive and healthy manner are those that take charge of their choice.

What are some of the reasons people accept or welcome change?

► Sometimes things are already bad and we want things to change for the better. If you are overloaded at work, if you have contention with peers or a boss, if you have poor working conditions, and so forth—a positive change is welcome.

► Sometimes the way we have been doing things gets boring or old. We change to get more variety and excitement in our personal and professional lives.

► It's natural to change. Sometimes we have changed just because it was the natural thing to do. When Yellowstone Park was devastated by fire we were all saddened, and yet just a few years later the park is coming back to life greener, younger, stronger, and healthier because of the cleansing fire. Many of us are like the fire in the park, when the change comes we initially perceive it as bad, but afterward everything seems to work out okay.

► Sometimes change is imposed upon us. We have no control over the change. So why not accept the change with a positive attitude? Sometimes people just realize it is not worth fighting the change and decide to quickly accept it in order to turn the situation into an opportunity instead of a loss.

► We become stronger and are challenged by change. Many people will take on a new challenge because it is an exciting and exhilarating challenge. Other changes make us stronger—for example, when we are out of shape and we begin to get ready for some athletic event, the first few workouts cause our muscles to become painful and sore. After the muscles heal they become stronger and more fine-tuned than they were. The initial pain and soreness is replaced with growth and strength.

CHANGE LEADERS

Change leaders—people who lead the way to accept change or innovation—tend to embrace and popularize many kinds of innovations that ultimately are accepted by the mainstream. Change leaders range in age from their 20s to 50s. Despite the diversity in age, they exhibit six consistent personality traits (MacEvoy, 1994). These people are:

> **Novelty-Seeking**
>
> **Stimulation-Seeking**
>
> **Information-Seeking**
>
> **Individualistic**
>
> **Sociable**
>
> **Fashionable**

These change leaders are more likely than average to use computers, video games, cable TV, cellular phones, and the like. They have a wide range of contacts in different occupational and social groups. They are physically vigorous and highly oriented to recreation and travel. They are also big users of print, broadcast, and electronic media. They also tend to accept more easily changes in organizational settings.

CHANGE AGENTS

In a broad sense anyone can be a change agent; however, in organizations today we often think in terms of "professional" and "nonprofessional" change agents. Professional change agents are of two kinds—those internal to the organization and those external to the organization. The professional change agents, whether internal or external to the organization, have this in common: They both are paid by the organization and their primary role is to help bring about positive changes within the organization.

Professional change agents are known by many different titles such as: organization development consultants, management consultants, organization systems designers, training specialists, community development consultants, educational methodologists, total quality specialists, and so on.

Nonprofessional change agents can be anyone in any job. The pace of change has become so rapid that more and more organizations are placing a greater emphasis on the need for every worker in any capacity to take an active role in managing the change in their jobs. Because of our own personal styles and preferences some of us will take on change-generator roles, whereas others of us will take on the change-implementor or change-adopter roles.

Because the trend continues to move toward increased change we will see more professional change agents working with organizations both as internal and external agents of change. We will also see more line managers increase the percentage of their job responsibilities that have to do with change management.

What Change Agents Do

In a broad sense, the change agent is involved in either generating, implementing, or adopting change. The change agent may be involved in doing any of the following:

- Identify what needs to be changed
- Convert the issue into a felt need
- Demonstrate support for a change
- Defend the change in its initial stages
- Develop the change processes needed to implement the change at various levels
- Commit to and adopt the change
- Maintain an ongoing level of change in order for the change to strengthen and grow
- Ingrain the change into the system until the new change becomes the norm, habit, or standard practice

CHANGE AGENTS (continued)

Change Agent Competencies

We can gain a better understanding of what change agents do by examining some of the competencies they are expected to exhibit. McBer and Company have developed a model of competencies for successful change agents. The model is primarily intended for business change agents but it has good applicability for change agents in any organizational setting. There are four major competencies in the model: interpersonal skills, diagnostic skills, initiation skills, and organizational skills. These skills and what they encompass are presented below.

Interpersonal-Skills Competencies

- The ability to express empathy

- Positive expectations of people

- Genuineness

Diagnostic-Skills Competencies

- Knowledge of the principles of individual and organizational development variables and systems

- The ability to collect meaningful data from individuals and organizational systems through such means as interviews, surveys, and observations

- The ability to draw conclusions from complex data and make accurate diagnoses

Initiation-Skills Competencies

- The ability to influence and market skills, and to identify and persuade prospective internal customers to use services

- The ability to make presentations in a concise, interesting, and informative manner

- The ability to manage groups and group dynamics

- The ability to engage in problem solving and planning, and to make recommendations and help customers with problem solving, goal setting, and planning to improve organizational performance

Organizational-Skills Competencies

- The ability to design adult-learning curricula and organizational development exercises

- The ability to administer resources such as personnel, materials, schedules, and training sites

Through the organizational and diagnostic skills the change agent plans and designs the work. Through the interpersonal and initiating skills the change agent implements the plans to accomplish the change.

Through the end of the book, we will follow the case study of Lauren, a marketing manager who seeks out an OD specialist.

CASE STUDY PART 1

The Change Agent

Lauren is the marketing department manager. She has noticed that her staff seems to be pulling in separate directions and some members have trouble cooperating with others. She feels team building will help her department function in a more positive and productive way.

Lauren interviews several OD consultants to find the change agent she thinks will be right for what she needs.

Lauren decides on Dale, an organization development consultant that best answered the question "How will this change agent build a group into a team?"

Dale meets with Lauren to discuss the problems. Dale and Lauren define the problem as Lauren sees it. They discuss specific questions to ask and data that will be collected from interviews with team members.

Dale interviews Lauren's staff and immediately a number of issues surface that appear counterproductive to effective functioning. Lack of communication is identified as the most serious problem, and many of the other major issues are the direct result of the communication breakdown.

Dale reports the general findings back to Lauren without mentioning any names. After discussing the problem and possible ways to solve it, they decided on a two-day team building retreat. The goal of the retreat is to get the group to work through the issues that are causing the biggest problems.

Before the retreat, Dale puts together an agenda and shares it with Lauren. Upon approval, the agenda is given to all group members. Dale purposefully leaves the agenda quite open so that the group will get more involved in the problem-solving process and gain greater ownership in the process of working to achieve positive and productive change.

P A R T

5

Interventions

OVERVIEW OF INTERVENTIONS

Interventions are the tools of the OD consultant. The "traditional" interventions are: organization, group, and individual. See the chart below. These interventions are covered in this Part. The "other" and "newer" interventions will be covered in Part 6.

OD Interventions

TRADITIONAL

INDIVIDUAL

- Third party
- Laboratory group training
- Career/life planning

GROUP

- Process consultation
- Family group team building
- Diagnostic team building
- Intergroup team building
- Organizational mirror

ORGANIZATION

- The confrontation meeting
- Survey/Feedback
- Environmental scanning

OTHER TRADITIONAL

- Grid OD
- Likert System 4
- Work redesign
- Outdoor laboratory training
- Role analysis technique

NEWER

- Quality circles
- Self-directed work teams
- Training exercises/games
- Electronic team building
- Organization transformation
- Total quality management
- Learning organizations
- Search conferences
- Performance management
- Appreciative inquiry
- Reengineering
- Transorganizational OD

THIRD-PARTY INTERVENTION

What Is It?

A consultant is usually asked to help in resolving issues when two individuals who have critical functions in an organization are not working well together and are having major conflict or disagreement. Because the conflict has grown to a level where the two parties cannot remain objective enough to resolve the conflict themselves, a third person or party becomes a mediator in the process to achieve resolution. The third party skillfully manages the issues so that each side can air their differences and work toward a successful solution without becoming overly emotional or counterproductive.

How Is It Done?

Like so many of the OD interventions, there may be a number of different ways to accomplish it. Here is a typical example of how a third-party intervention is accomplished:

 The third party (consultant) is asked to help solve the conflict between two individuals.

 The consultant contacts the individuals and sets up interviews with each. In the interviews the consultant finds out the nature of the perceived problems and sets the ground rules for resolving the issues.

 Each party is asked to give the problem serious thought, and write down their answers, to these critical areas:

- What would you like your relationship to be like ideally?

- What positives do you see in the other person?

- What has the person done to cause you pain or keep you from being as effective as you would like to be in doing your work?

- What could the other party do more of?

- What could the other party do less of or stop doing?

- Finally, looking at all of the above questions, how would you predict the other party will answer these questions?

When they meet, each of the parties shares their answers to the question in #3 above. Typically, the third-party consultant keeps them on track here and helps them focus only on clarifying and gaining an understanding of the other party's views.

In this step, the two parties begin to work out solutions and plans for the future regarding how they can accommodate the expectations of the other party. The consultant may facilitate the discussion by helping them to write agreed-upon action plans on an easel, again clarifying the details for maximum understanding.

Once the plan is agreed to by both parties, follow-up dates are set to assess progress and make the necessary course corrections.

PROS

► In some cases a team cannot progress because of the poor relationship of two key people. This is an excellent intervention to clear up that key relationship prior to the entire team engaging in team building.

► A "win-win" outcome leads to a tremendous release of positive energy toward productive gains, not just for the parties involved, but for all other co-workers as well.

THIRD-PARTY INTERVENTION (continued)

► The parties are sometimes not ready emotionally and mentally to resolve the issues. Instead, they choose to continue to be angry, hurt, or engage in in otherwise counterproductive behavior.

► At times the third party may be perceived as not being objective enough or taking sides. At other times, people don't want to air their dirty laundry with a third party.

► One or both of the parties may have a hidden agenda that throws the process off course and keeps it from being successful.

Other Comments and Ideas

• It is a good idea to set up the meeting on neutral ground.

• The third party is a major key to success; they must be credible and acceptable to both parties and highly skilled in conflict management.

• Remember, most conflicts can be handled between two people themselves. This process is just for those situations where conflict has grown to a significant level and can't be worked out any other way.

LABORATORY GROUPS

What Is It?

This intervention has also been referred to as a "T-group" or "sensitivity group." This was one of the first interventions in OD. Essentially a group of between 10 and 15 people, along with one or two experienced consultants, meets to learn about group dynamics and their own individual styles and relationships. The data for the discussion is derived from the interactions and things said and done by each member of the group at the time of the meeting. So someone in the group says something, and someone else reacts to how it was said and how it may have impacted them, and so on. This is the reason it is referred to as a laboratory group—because the experience is as if you are in a group laboratory examining how you come across to others, how you give and receive feedback, perceive others' reactions, deal with different personalities, and learn about your own behaviors in these circumstances.

The group may meet for a day or two, or as long as several weeks. The consultants may at times share insights about group and personality theory and practice, but for the main part the actual experiences that occur between the participants themselves form the basis for learning, growing, and changing.

How Is It Done?

Usually a person (or group) becomes aware that they could use an experience to help them look at how their behaviors impact themselves and people they work with.

An individual could go to a laboratory group by themself and not know anyone else prior to going. This is known as a *stranger group.* When an entire group of people that works together on a daily basis attends a laboratory group, it is called a *family group.* When a family group goes through a process like this, it is usually the first step in a larger plan to do some extensive team building.

The T-group or laboratory experience is so unstructured that it is difficult to really assign any linear arrangement. However, here are some general steps:

 Individuals sign up for a T-group at the National Training Laboratories or other such training organization.

LABORATORY GROUPS (continued)

They are assigned to a group with 10 or 15 other people from various organizations, along with a professional facilitator/trainer of group dynamics.

Typically the facilitator starts out with introductions and explains that his/her role is to be a resource to the group. After that the trainer becomes silent.

The group then begins to struggle with how to proceed. The group deals with who will be the leader, what will be the agenda, and what is the purpose of being there.

As the group struggles along, they begin giving feedback to each other on how they are coming across. They examine more productive ways to interact.

Occasionally the trainer may interject to help the group deal with issues or insights that will maximize the learning experience and encourage open and productive discussion.

PROS

► People can learn invaluable lessons about how they handle interpersonal relations with others.

► Individuals learn a great deal about group dynamics, handling conflict, collaboration, competition, leadership styles, blind spots, hidden agendas, etc.

► Participants can learn a great deal about listening skills and how to process and respond to feedback from others.

C O N S

▶ For some people the experience is too personal and too threatening. They are just not ready for it.

▶ The mechanisms for follow up, particularly within the organization, are limited.

▶ Fears and misconceptions about T-groups are widespread.

▶ In some cases the experience is "hit or miss." You may or may not have a deep learning experience depending on the way things happen and how much you are personally willing to risk.

Other Comments and Ideas

• It is very important that individuals voluntarily enter into the laboratory experience. If people are not ready for this type of personal feedback and confrontation, it could backfire.

• If people are overly stressed or have had serious emotional problems this may just make things worse. The assumption is that individuals attending the T-group have a reasonable level of stamina and maturity to handle serious interpersonal feedback and introspection.

CAREER/LIFE PLANNING

What Is It?

This is an intervention that helps individuals take greater ownership and control of both their personal life and career goals. One of the basic assumptions of OD is that when systems are in alignment they will be more productive. In this case, the principle applies to the individual's goals aligning with the organization's goals for greater synergy and success. The process is to identify where you are now, where you want to be, and how you plan to close the gap.

How Is It Done?

There are a number of different ways to accomplish this intervention. Usually an organization that has some savvy about this intervention has been educated by a consultant about the importance of both the organization and the individuals within the organization. The organization will sometimes choose to set up a workshop that runs on a regular basis for which individuals can voluntarily sign up. Sometimes a facilitator is invited to conduct the intervention for the entire group at one time. Here are some typical steps in the process:

The manager shares the purpose and objectives of the meeting. She/he then turns the time over to the consultant.

The consultant gives an overview of the process they are about to go through and helps the group to identify general ground rules.

The consultant divides the members into pairs or small groups. Each individual answers key questions, while the other person(s) acts as advisor.

Several key questions are put on a flipchart for each individual to answer in turn. Here are some typical questions:

- What are your most valuable skills and personal assets?

- What have been your most notable accomplishments and experiences?

- If you could do anything you want to do in your career/life what would it be?

- What people would you like most to respect you in your career/life, and what qualities would you want them to respect you for?

- Which of those qualities do you have today?

- How can you obtain those you don't already have?

- If you were the Chairman of the Board of a company whose sole product is you, picture a board meeting where you have assembled your directors (the people you respect the most in your life). Who would you want to be around the table at the meeting, and why?

- If you could hear what people say about you when you die, what would you like them to say?

- If money were no object, what would you really like to do with your time?

- If the organization would let you make three major contributions with your talents and abilities over the next three to five years, what would they be?

- If you could only make one contribution to your family, organization, career, society, etc. over the next six months, what would it be?

- What are your five major goals for your profession, job, significant others, life, etc., in the next 5 to 10 years? What resources will you need to achieve them? What barriers will you have to eliminate before you can achieve them?

The pairs now share their answers to the questions and help each other clarify why they answered as they did. Partners help by running reality checks in some cases and encouraging others to have more self-confidence. Partners also look for recurring themes that give revealing data about what the person really wants to do. They may also point out incongruencies in goals.

CAREER/LIFE PLANNING (continued)

 Next, they help each other set some priorities for each of their goals.

 The next step is to set up a detailed action plan for achieving each goal and when.

 Partners set up follow-up checkpoints to encourage and support goal achievement.

PROS

► This is an excellent way for an organization or a manager to send a message that people are as important as tasks, capital equipment, or profits.

► It is an intervention that can truly be self-empowering.

► It builds stronger alignment between the individual and the organization.

► It unleashes new energy and potential for both the individual and the organization.

CONS

► Some people may decide that their goals are not congruent with the organization and leave.

► If the client is doing this to manipulate individuals into early retirement or in some other direction they do not want to go, it will often backfire.

Other Comments and Ideas

- This type of intervention can be done in a day or two at one time, or it could be divided into one or two hours a week, giving time between weeks for more introspection and clarity. Be sure to allow time for follow-up.

- For those concerned about losing good people, you are going to lose good people anyway. You may as well ensure a great future for the majority that stay, instead of worrying about the minority that leave.

- This particular intervention has led to numerous career/life planning exercises, books, consulting firms, and associations specializing in this area alone.

PROCESS CONSULTATION

What Is It?

Process consultation may be the most widely used intervention in OD. It is typically an ongoing intervention (or at least comprises a series of meetings) used with a number of workgroups in the organization to help them improve their interpersonal and group processes. In process consultation, the consultant observes individuals and groups in action, helping them learn to diagnose and solve their own problems. The consultant will usually focus on group roles and norms, problem-solving and decision-making skills, leadership styles, power and authority, feedback and listening skills.

How Is It Done?

There is no standard way of doing process consultation. What may be appropriate in one circumstance will not work in another situation; however, here are some typical steps of this intervention:

The organization sees the need to improve its group process skills in order to improve overall performance, so an internal or external consultant is brought in to help.

After normal contracting, the consultant begins to observe the processes between individuals and workgroups within the organization.

As the consultant works with the organization, he or she will use a variety of microinterventions such as listening, probing, questioning, clarifying, reflecting, synthesizing, and summarizing. He or she helps the group by interjecting comments and ideas on how to improve the work by answering key questions such as:

- How well are you accomplishing the group task roles of seeking and giving information, asking questions, summarizing, seeking input and listening, and so forth?

- How well are you accomplishing the maintenance roles such as gatekeeping, compromising, harmonizing, supporting, encouraging, and so forth?

- How well are you solving problems and making decisions? And what are the processes you are using to solve problems and make decisions? Are these processes effective?

- How well have you set up your group norms and rules to help guide your functioning as a productive group?

- How well are you dealing with power and authority in the group?

- What styles of leadership are being used and how effectively?

Other interventions used in process consultation include coaching and counseling individuals on more effective interpersonal styles, giving guidance and feedback on how to improve meeting agendas and processes, giving suggestions on how to improve group structures such as communication patterns, allocation of work, roles, responsibilities, and lines of authority.

PROS

► Process consultation has been a very effective intervention for improving existing workgroups' overall performance.

► The consultant models the behaviors he/she expects the clients to use; for example, to be an excellent teacher.

► Most of the microinterventions used by the consultant have high face validity, meaning they make intuitive sense and have good credibility among the clients.

PROCESS CONSULTATION (continued)

C O N S

▶ The process does take time, and some clients may get impatient.

▶ The goal of process consultation is to develop in the participants themselves many of the skills the consultant is using so that they will continue to solve their own problems and make their own decisions. Sometimes they don't get enough experience using the skills to continue to use them after the consultant's contract is finished.

▶ It can be costly and it is difficult to obtain measurable results.

Other Comments and Ideas

• This intervention is usually a forerunner of, or used in conjunction with, other interventions such as family group and intergroup team building, self-directed work teams, quality circles, and other interventions.

• Many of the same skills used in process consultation are used in all the other OD interventions.

• To those just starting to develop skills in OD, you would be wise to find ways to develop process consultation because it employs fundamental skills used in, or related to, so many of the OD interventions.

WHAT IS FAMILY GROUP TEAM BUILDING? READ ON TO FIND OUT!

FAMILY GROUP TEAM BUILDING

What Is It?

Team building is an intervention where a work group attempts to improve its effectiveness and performance by focusing on its norms and procedures, problem- and decision-making processes, interpersonal relationships and group processes, goals and strategies, structures and tasks, culture, leadership style, and related areas. There are several types of team building and interventions, but the two most widely known are Family Group Team Building (FTB) and Diagnostic Team Building (DTB). In Diagnostic Team Building, the group's purpose is only to diagnose the problems and opportunities. In Family Team Building they will not just diagnose, but also move on to the action-solution mode.

At times the interventions are categorized according to their focus, such as a temporary work team, a new work team or new team member, a specific task team, etc. Nearly all team building simultaneously examines ways to improve not only *what* the team is working on—the task—but *how* the team is working on the task—the process. Improving performance in both areas at the same time makes the team building intervention a powerful one.

Since there are some key differences between a Family Group Team Building intervention and a Diagnostic Team Building intervention we will look at FTB first and DTB next.

How Is It Done?

There are a variety of ways to conduct FTB. Here are some of the typical steps:

FTB begins with some perceived need by the manager and other members of the work team. Some dysfunctional performance needs to be changed or some positive performance needs to be strengthened.

The manager of the team (who is typically the client) meets with the consultant and identifies a few basic objectives and outlines in general what he/she would like to accomplish. The consultant and the client decide upon the basic ground rules.

FAMILY GROUP TEAM BUILDING (continued)

 Next is the initial data collection phase. Most of the data is collected by individual interviews, observation, and questionnaires. The consultant and the client decide in advance if the team will keep the information sources confidential or share who said what when they get together later.

 The consultant analyzes and summarizes the data, usually into major themes and categories. As mentioned before, the data can be anonymous or clearly identified as to source.

 Some type of preliminary meeting is held prior to the team building meeting. The consultant will meet with the client to review the general findings and jointly plan the team building meeting(s). In other cases, the manager, consultant, and several key members of the team may have a preliminary planning meeting to review the purpose, goals, objectives, and general outline for the meeting with the team.

 Typically, a team building meeting is held anywhere from one day to three days initially. The meeting is usually held off-site in a place where all team members can focus their attention on the purpose of the meeting. These are some common steps that occur at the meeting:

- The manager welcomes the team and restates the purpose of the meeting and turns the time over to the consultant.

- The consultant facilitates a discussion of the objectives of the meeting and helps the team set up ground rules on how they will deal with both task and process issues.

- The consultant then reviews the findings of the data from the interviews or other sources of data.

- The issues are then prioritized in the order they will be worked on. Both process and task issues are prioritized; in some cases, the team may have to clarify the issues and recategorize the issues before they can prioritize.

- They begin to work through the issues to identify ways they can improve their performance. The consultant facilitates as needed to help the group learn from the experience of the moment as well as past experience. Consultants use many of the same skills that are used in process consultation.

- For each issue that is on the list, the team will make an action plan including who will do what specific task and when.

- Follow up meeting(s) are planned to ensure that action plans are being carried out. Course corrections are made if schedules are not met to reevaluate and stay focused on achieving desired outcomes.

STEP 7 The actual follow-up and evaluative meetings are held as planned. The follow-up meetings may lead to another set of team building meetings at an even more sophisticated and productive level. Eventually the team develops many, if not all, of the consultant's facilitative skills so they can carry on the growth cycle themselves.

PROS

► This is an excellent way to focus the entire group on the problem or opportunity.

► It maximizes the synergy of the team as they work toward the goal.

► In some studies of OD, the team building intervention was found to be the most effective intervention.

► It can develop skills and relationships that will become a new high-performance standard of excellence for the participating team as well as for other teams to emulate.

► For some teams, it's the first time they have ever focused on process skills, which work alongside of good task skills.

FAMILY GROUP TEAM BUILDING (continued)

CONS

▶ Dealing effectively with process issues can take a great deal of time. If you can't take the time to bring closure, think twice about starting in the first place.

▶ This can be extremely risky for a manager, or other members of the team, who have developed a lot of resentment from other team members. You will need a skillful consultant to make this a "win-win" situation.

▶ Teams may be changing so fast that it is difficult to build a maximum level of effectiveness over the long haul.

Other Comments and Ideas

• It is best if all team members reach consensus that they want to participate in a team building intervention. You can make it mandatory to come to the meetings, but let people otherwise respond within the limits of their abilities.

• Some people are so task oriented that it is difficult to experience the process side of the equation without some major pain and ambiguity.

• Team building has become more important in recent years because of the emphasis on letting teams design ways of achieving maximum performance.

• Team building is not for everyone. If team members primarily work alone, or have no real need to work together, then it may be counterproductive.

DIAGNOSTIC TEAM BUILDING

What Is It?

Diagnostic Team Building (DTB) is an intervention used to identify the problems and opportunities of a team. Although it can be done without a consultant, typically a consultant is used to help facilitate the meeting. The manager and consultant usually meet before the meeting to discuss the purpose and agenda. Usually the manager and/or consultant will also meet with some or all of the team members in advance of the meeting to get their input and give them some idea of what will take place.

There are a number of different variations to this intervention. Here are the typical steps:

Preliminary meetings are held with the manager, team members, and the consultant if one is involved. In some cases, the specific agenda items are determined in these advance meetings so the team members have more time to prepare their thoughts for the diagnostic meeting.

The diagnostic team building meeting is held. Typically, it is one day in length. Here's how the meeting might unfold:

- The manager makes a few opening remarks, including an overview of the meeting, the purpose, ground rules, and roles. The manager will then act as the meeting facilitator or turn the time over to the consultant to facilitate the meeting.

- If it has not been done previously, the team is now given on a flipchart a few key questions that will be answered by the team, such as:

    "What are the things we are doing well as a team?"
    (Look at both the task and relationship areas.)

    "What are the things we need to do to improve as a team?"
    (Look at both the task and relationship areas.)

- The team is given time to answer the questions. This can be done in any of several different ways. Options A or B are recommended in order to get maximum involvement and ownership in the process:

DIAGNOSTIC TEAM BUILDING (continued)

A. The total group can answer the questions together.

B. The group can be subdivided into smaller groups to address the questions.

C. The group can be divided into pairs to come up with answers.

- Next, the group (or subgroups/pairs) discusses the data: clarifying, categorizing, and prioritizing the areas that need to be addressed.

- The final step is to set up some plan of how action will be taken to address the issues. This usually entails more extensive team building meeting(s) later on to resolve the issues.

 At least one follow-up meeting is set up to bring closure if plans have not already been made to create action teams to address the issues.

PROS

▶ This is a good way to get everyone involved in the process of identifying what barriers are impeding the group's performance.

▶ It is a good way to get an overview of the entire scope of problems with which the team may have to deal.

▶ This is a good way to lead up to a team building session. It's less risky, because all you are doing is identifying the problems and making some recommendations on how to go about solving them. It's a good way to prepare for team building or other interventions that may require more personal energy, time, and maturity.

CONS

► The first time around this type of intervention may be overwhelming because there is a backlog of problems to deal with. For groups that don't have good processes in place to diagnose and address problems, this may figuratively open the floodgates.

► If you are not willing to set up action plans to resolve the problems that surface in the meeting, then it is best not to start in the first place.

► This is just the beginning of the process of problem solving for the team. There is still a lot of work ahead to achieve performance successes.

Other Comments and Ideas

• This is a good intervention to use for temporary task force teams to get things rolling.

• Every team should ideally spend a day or a half-day every six to eight months diagnosing where they are and where they are going.

• Again, this is only a diagnostic meeting to begin the process. Taking specific action is reserved for later, but you should follow up soon so you will not lose your momentum or cause people to lose faith in the process.

INTERGROUP TEAM BUILDING

What Is It?

This intervention is used to build the working relationship between two teams. The best use of this intervention is in those situations where teams have a great deal of interdependence in their work. For example, some production teams cannot do their work without the help of engineering, etc. At times, critical departments or groups will build up unhealthy perceptions, communications, and competition that will cause performance to drop. This intervention can help to get the teams working in greater harmony and cohesiveness. Many of the same principles that apply to a family team apply here as well. Instead of improving working relations between individuals within a group, you are improving working relations between teams.

How Is It Done?

Like many other interventions there are numbers of ways this could be done. Here is a typical way of doing it:

Usually the process starts with someone seeing that things aren't working well between two units. In turn, the managers of the two teams believe that things could be better, and they get together to discuss ways to improve the working relationship. If a consultant is involved, she or he will be brought in at this point in the process. They will discuss how and when to set up the intervention meeting.

The managers then meet with their respective teams to get input and give them some idea of what will be accomplished and when the meeting will be held.

The meeting is held and goes as follows:

- The managers of the departments give a brief introduction and outline for the meeting. Either the consultant or the managers conduct the meeting. The meeting facilitator will begin by laying down a few ground rules.

- Next, the facilitator will introduce a few key questions for each team to answer such as:

  "What are the things about the other group that you think they do well?"

  "What are the things you would like to see them do differently that would improve your working relationship?"

  "List how you think the other group will answer the above two questions?" For example, 'We think they will say they do _____ well.' Or, 'We think they will say we should be doing _____ differently.' "

- The teams are given flipchart paper and sent into separate rooms to answer the questions.

- The teams return with their answers and each team reads their answers. At this point, debate is not allowed. Questions can be asked to clarify what things mean so everyone has a clear understanding.

- The teams return to their rooms to do two things. First, they discuss what they have learned about how they were perceived; and second, they build a list of issues that need to be resolved. They also prioritize the list.

- The teams return and share their lists once again with each other. Then they begin to work together to come up with a combined list of issues that need to be addressed and they prioritize this list. Next, they set up action plans, make assignments, and set deadlines for resolution of the issues.

- Finally, the teams set up a follow-up meeting.

A follow-up meeting is held to assess how things are going and to make any course corrections to stay on track until goals are achieved.

INTERGROUP TEAM BUILDING (continued)

PROS

► This is a good way to get people from different teams working together to improve the performance of both teams.

► It can eliminate miscommunications, misperceptions, and misunderstandings that may have caused barriers to successful operations.

► It is a good way to get the teams focusing on competition outside of the organization instead of between themselves.

► It can do a great deal to empower everyone rather than leaving the burden of responsibility to only the managers.

CONS

► A skilled consultant will be needed if the groups are extremely hostile and also have weak conflict-resolution skills.

► Be sure to allow enough time to resolve and work through the issues. Cutting the discussion too short may be unhealthy and leave things unresolved.

► If you don't follow-up and complete the action plans, you may lose credibility, and the intervention could be counterproductive.

Other Comments and Ideas

• In some situations you will need to do some major work prior to this intervention. For example, if there is a lack of group process skills, then team building or process consultation may be needed before the meeting.

• The meetings usually last one or two days depending on the situation.

• This can also be used very effectively in cases where two new groups are forced to work together, such as in a merger or acquisition.

• The emphasis throughout the process should be on achieving a win-win situation. The group should keep focusing on how to overcome misperceptions and how these may have come about in the first place. It is important to determine effective ways to avoid future misperceptions.

ORGANIZATIONAL MIRROR

What Is It?

The Organizational Mirror is an intervention used to help a group or department (for example, accounting, sales, customer service, etc.) to get valuable feedback from other departments within the organization. A meeting is held to get honest feedback, in which the goal is to take a look in the "mirror" at yourself (as a department) as other departments see you. Many times when this intervention is used the department looking for feedback has already identified that it is having difficulty working with one or more of the other departments. Or, the host department may just want to improve its working relationships in general.

How Is It Done?

Usually a consultant is asked to help improve the relationships and effectiveness of the department, whose members can see that they would benefit from a better working relationship with one or more departments they work with on a regular basis.

The other departments are contacted and asked to send a couple of representatives to the meeting. Prior to the meeting, the consultant interviews the meeting participants to identify and clarify the issues/concerns and then the consultant summarizes the data for the meeting.

The meeting is held and basically follows these steps:

 There is a brief introduction by the meeting leader who outlines the agenda and purposes of the meetings, and ground rules are established.

 The consultant reviews the data from the interviews.

ORGANIZATIONAL MIRROR (continued)

 The outside departments form a *fishbowl* with the host department, or insiders, to discuss the issues.

What is a fishbowl? It's a meeting where two circles of people are formed. The inside circle takes the active role of discussing the topic at hand while the outside circle looks on to observe and listen. Usually the circles will switch back and forth, with inside to outside circles reversing the roles in order to give both groups an opportunity to actively share and hear the issues.

 The host department discusses what they heard and identifies any areas that need clarification.

 The consultant leads a general discussion to clarify and focus on the top issues. In some cases the groups are sent off by themselves to continue the discussion.

 Subgroups are formed, comprised of a mixture of host and outside departments, to identify the critical issues.

 The subgroups return after a time and report their perceptions.

 The entire group spends time identifying and prioritizing the issues.

 The subgroups return again to a breakout room where they set up specific action plans to address the issues. (This is sometimes done with the entire main group instead of breakout groups.)

STEP 10 The subgroups return and give reports of their proposed action plans.

STEP 11 The entire group plans the next follow-up meeting(s) to assess progress and stay on track until the plan has been accomplished.

PROS

► In a short period of time valuable feedback is collected, and issues can sometimes be clarified on the spot.

► This method improves the working relationships between departments.

► It opens the communication lines between departments.

► Outside departments take more ownership in the successes of the host department.

CONS

► Only the representatives to the meeting from the outside department may have ownership and change their attitudes toward the host department.

► People may not follow through with the action plans, especially those from outside the department where people have their own jobs to do.

► People may not be ready yet to invest, emotionally or otherwise, the time in this process to do it correctly.

► You need a skilled consultant to manage the process and keep it on track.

Other Comments and Ideas

- Usually you will limit the number of people to around 20.

- Although this could take as little as four hours, it usually takes a day or more.

- In organizations that have adopted a philosophy that every other department should be treated as an "internal customer," this is an excellent way to get feedback from them.

- You will want to pick representatives from the outside departments that are well respected and can do a good job of influencing their departments about the proposed changes and plans.

CONFRONTATION MEETING

What Is It?

The confrontation meeting is an intervention where the organization meets for about a day to set goals to improve the organization's health and establish a direction for change. This involves a large group—in some cases over a hundred people are involved. In smaller organizations this may include the entire organization, and in larger organizations it may only involve a representative sampling of the various parts of the organization. The meeting usually lasts one day.

How Is It Done?

Usually top management of the organization realizes that one or more problems that are causing organizational stress. They want to solve the problems or issues quickly with maximum involvement from all parts of the organization, so they call a meeting. In the meeting the following steps take place:

The meeting leader, usually someone from top management, begins the meeting and states the goals and objectives for the meeting. At this point either the meeting leader or the consultant will lay out the ground rules, such as encouraging open and honest discussion without fear of reprisal.

The large group is then divided into smaller subgroups of between five to eight people per group. The subgroups should be composed of the best mixture possible of the various parts of the organization. No one should have their boss in the same group; usually the top management is a separate subgroup.

For about an hour the subgroups identify the things that need to be examined both personally and organizationally to improve the organization's health; for example, policies and procedures, attitudes, unrealistic goals, lack of resources, trust, teamwork, etc. The list of items is summarized by each group on a flipchart, and someone from the group reports the results in the next session.

4 All the subgroups reconvene into one large group, and each subgroup reports back their list of problems and issues. The meeting leader or consultant then categorizes the lists into several major categories. This is usually followed by a break while time is taken to duplicate the lists for everyone at the meeting.

5 Next, the larger group is once again divided into subgroups, but this time the subgroups are composed of the functional departments or areas from the organization such as MIS, accounting, sales, engineering, etc. This subgroup is lead by the functional manager of the area. Each group is given a three-part charge:

- Discuss the problems and issues relating to your area or department and prioritize them. Then determine a plan of action to solve the problems including timetables.

- Identify and prioritize the problems and concerns top management should be dealing with.

- Set up a plan to communicate and involve those members of the organization who are not present at the meeting.

6 The groups reconvene to report back to the main group their answers and action plans.

7 The meeting leader and other top management give their initial reactions to the plans. They set up a follow-up meeting with the entire group.

8 Top management meets to set up plans of action to address the issues raised in the meeting. Functional groups also meet to ensure that follow-up action is being achieved.

CONFRONTATIONAL MEETING (continued)

STEP 9 Four to six weeks later a follow-up meeting is held with the entire group to report progress on each action plan and to make course corrections as needed.

PROS

► This is a quick way to improve the organization's health.

► It improves communication at all levels of the organization.

► It maximizes ownership and commitment to organization improvement.

CONS

► This method will backfire if plans are not carried out.

► It will be thwarted if top management doesn't support the process and follow-up actions.

► It may be hard to get everyone together at the same time and place.

► It may be costly to have everyone together for a day especially if the organization's members are spread out geographically.

Other Comments and Ideas

• This intervention takes excellent planning and coordination. Most organizations never do it because it is such a major effort.

• There is greater risk and greater gain.

• It will probably not solve problems with management style and other critical relationship issues.

• This intervention can have a major impact in a *very* short amount of time.

SURVEY/FEEDBACK

What Is It?

Survey/Feedback has sometimes been referred to as attitude survey or survey research, and is one of the fundamental interventions of OD. Typically, a questionnaire is designed to collect organizational data in every area of the organization. Feedback is given on how members perceive a number of areas such as superior-subordinate relations, leadership, communications, pay, benefits, training, career development, customer service, quality, and performance in general. Essentially, it is like getting a physical examination to check on your overall health.

In a nutshell, it is a process of

- Identifying the areas of organizational health that need to be assessed

- Designing the questionnaire

- Collecting the data

- Analyzing and interpreting the data

- Feeding back the data

- Taking action steps to respond to the data

How Is It Done?

Credit is given to the University of Michigan's Institute of Social Research for outlining the steps in this process, which are typically as follows:

1 The top management of the unit or organization believes an intervention is in order to check the health of the organization. They, in turn, are involved from the onset in planning how the process will be conducted within the organization. Usually a consultant is involved in the process of planning, and will also be the one who either selects an existing survey instrument or develops one to meet the needs of the particular client organization.

90

SURVEY/FEEDBACK (continued)

 A meeting is often set up to share with the department managers what the objectives of the survey are to be and answer any questions and concerns about the process. Each of the managers is given a copy of the survey instrument to review and complete themselves.

 The survey is distributed and completed by organization members. Usually a couple of weeks is given as a deadline to return the surveys. The surveys are anonymous but identified by department or working unit.

 When the surveys are completed and returned, the consultant compiles and analyzes the data and begins the process of feeding back the data.

 The consultant gives top management an overview of, and teaches them how to interpret, the data for their respective departments. The consultant will also set up a time to help train other managers to conduct the process.

 Meetings are held to train leaders on how to interpret and feed back the data as well as set up action plans to resolve the issues.

 Meetings are then held at every level within each department or unit to feed back and react to the data.

 In the same meeting as #7 above, or at a separate follow-up meeting, the department or unit sets up action plans to resolve any additional issues that have surfaced in the feedback meeting itself.

STEP 9 At some point in the future, usually six months to a year, the survey is conducted again to see if any improvement has been made. The first survey is used as a baseline measure to compare with the next survey. The organization can then decide to start the process over in a continuing effort to improve performance.

PROS

► This intervention gets the entire unit/organization involved in the improvement process.

► When everyone gets involved from the top on down, there can be an immediate and major impact on the performance of the organization.

► It is a good way to measure the overall health of the organization, identifying the cancers and cutting them out, or preventing them from getting out of hand or starting in the first place.

CONS

► There may be a dip in overall productivity for a time while the organization works toward the new performance level.

► If people distrust management or fear retribution, they may be afraid to answer honestly or may not even send in the survey, thwarting the entire process.

► If managers lack the skills necessary in the feedback and action planning process, the overall success of the process is sometimes impeded.

Other Comments and Ideas

• In some cases, organizations will have a consultant at the feedback meetings to help facilitate the process. A skilled facilitator can be an immense help in these situations.

• For most effective results, the survey feedback intervention should be used in combination with other OD interventions.

• It is important to turn feedback around quickly. I know of one situation where it took over six months to give feedback, by which time it had no credibility and people felt strong resentment toward the process.

OPEN SYSTEMS PLANNING

What Is It?

Open Systems Planning (OPS) is an intervention that helps the organization assess the impact that external environments have on them.

By *external environments,* we are referring to all major outside influences on the organization. There are all kinds of influences that are constantly impacting an organization that must be addressed in order for it to stay healthy. Some of those influences might be:

- Government regulations

- Stockholders

- Clients/Customers

- Employees and other company departments

- Outside suppliers and vendors

- Distribution and transportation channels

- Communication and electronic systems

- Other governments

- Sources of raw materials

- Special interest groups and associations

All of these forces can have an influence on how an organization will function in the present and future. And, there are others. If we are talking about a smaller entity, such as a division of a larger company, then we would have to include all the other departments and internal functions of the organization. Because this intervention looks at the impact of external environments, this intervention is sometimes referred to as *environmental scanning.*

How Is It Done?

Essentially this is a process of identifying who or what external influences exist, and then brainstorming realistic present and future scenario states of the organization, including any action plans the organization could take to create those scenarios. Here are some of the typical steps that might be taken in this intervention.

Usually the client (top manager) and the consultant have discussed the need for such an intervention, along with the potential benefits. This leads to the manager getting input from key managers and individuals within the organization.

A meeting is set up to accomplish the planning and goes something like this:

- The manager explains the purpose and objectives for the meeting and gives an overview of the process. The consultant then addresses the group to help them identify the ground rules and get started.

- The group makes a list (like the one on page 92) of all the different outside influences acting on the client organization (the "present state scenario" list). Then they brainstorm all the expectations these groups have for their organization.

- Next, the group analyzes and assesses how well they are currently responding to these expectations and demands.

- Then the group examines the organization's behaviors, actions, and beliefs to see if it can identify what really makes the organization tick. What does it really stand for? What is its true identity? What are its core values? What is its mission and purpose?

- In the next step, the group is asked to create the "realistic future state scenario" list. Here they ask and answer questions like, "If we didn't make any changes to our present state of operations, what will we realistically look like in the future?"

OPEN SYSTEMS PLANNING (continued)

- Next, they address the same kind of question about the "ideal future state." "What would we ideally like to see our future state be?"

- In the next step the group compares the present state with the ideal future state. They then put together action plans to alter their course to achieve the desired outcome.

STEP 3 Follow-up meetings are held to assess progress toward the goals in the plan.

PROS

▶ This intervention keeps organizations from getting blindsided. At times organizations get so focused in a narrow direction, they don't look up until they have a hit a tree in the road.

▶ This is a good way to get a reality check on how well you are meeting the expectations of the critical stakeholders of your organization.

▶ It can give new energy and synergy to the organization as you redefine yourselves as an organization and focus on a new shared vision of the future.

▶ It may very well be your ticket to survival as an organization.

CONS

▶ Make sure you have identified all the key influences. Leaving a key factor out may derail the plans later on.

▶ You must have the commitment and energy to follow through; otherwise, you will have wasted valuable discussion time. This is a time-consuming process, and while it can net you some excellent rewards, you must give it enough time to do it right or it is best not to do it at all.

Other Comments and Ideas

- A good consultant/facilitator can be invaluable in helping you to stay on track and keep focused on what your final goals are.

- Things are changing so rapidly in our environment today, it's probably a good idea to do this intervention at least once a year for your organization.

CASE STUDY PART 2

The Intervention

At the beginning of the retreat, Dale starts by sharing the feedback from the data-collection interviews. She then gives a summary of the main themes and issues that kept recurring in the interviews. Ground rules of the retreat are to be open, honest, objective and to participate.

The group lists and prioritizes the issues in terms of what would have the greatest positive impact on the group if it was changed. They decide communication is the top issue, then break the issue of communication into several sub-issues.

In small groups, the issues are tackled in problem-solving groups one at a time. Groups brainstorm with the goal of identifying the three best solutions. The small groups then re-form back into the whole group and share ideas to see what solutions they might have in common. Dale facilitates the discussion and brings the group to clarification on several points.

As each point is clarified, she helps the group list who will do what and when to ensure that the behavior change takes place and that communication behaviors actually change for the better.

PART

6

Other OD Interventions

MORE OD INTERVENTIONS

There are a few other traditional OD interventions that should be discussed, although in less detail than those in the preceding section. These are Grid OD, Likert's System 4, Work Redesign, Outdoor Laboratory Training, and Role Analysis Technique.

This section will also present interventions that have evolved from strong OD foundations and are considered to be the next generation of OD. These interventions are Quality Circles, Self-Directed Teams, Training Exercises and Games, Electronic Team Building, Organizational Transformation, Total Quality Management, Learning Organizations, Search Conferences, Performance Management, Appreciative Inquiry, Reengineering, and Transorganizational OD.

Grid OD

Grid OD is an organization-wide systems change intervention that includes a host of other interventions to achieve organizational excellence. The intervention may take several years to complete. It has six major phases:

1. **The Managerial Grid Seminar**

2. **Team Development**

3. **Intergroup Development**

4. **Development of the Ideal Strategic Organization Model**

5. **Implementing the Ideal Strategic Model**

6. **Organization-Wide Measurement and Evaluation**

MORE OD INTERVENTIONS (continued)

Likert System 4

Much of the early work by Rensis Likert was the development of a 105-item intervention survey that focused on a variety of organizational climate variables such as leadership, communication, decision making, job satisfaction, and peer relations.

The survey assesses four overall styles of participative leadership and organizational climate on a continuum from 1 to 4. In system 1, the organization is more controlling, and participation in decision making is limited to the top management. Systems 2, 3, and 4 progress away from this state—to where system 4 is much more open, participative and empowering, and decision making is a shared responsibility.

Work Redesign

The concept of Work Redesign is to increase performance and job satisfaction by finding new ways to design work. Oftentimes the outcome of this intervention is a significant increase in productivity on the part of workers.

The intervention starts with a thorough diagnosis of a work unit or units. The consultant in this situation has some basic principles that guide success. Typically, the goal is to do the following:

- Get more autonomy back into the work

- Get people closer to the customers

- Get interrelated tasks grouped together

- Get people to feel greater responsibility and accountability for their work

- Give people measurable feedback indicators so they know how they are doing and can gauge their own performance

- Give people a bigger picture and knowledge of the actual work results

- Maximize the workers' skills and abilities

- Eliminate unnecessary tasks and increase the significance of each task that remains

Outdoor Laboratory Training

Outdoor Laboratory Training is a form of team building that typically revolves around some type of outdoor adventure. But the basic goals of improving the team are still the same as in any team building situation. These labs have been called by a variety of other names such as "ropes", adventure learning, and wilderness labs. The teams experience some adventurous activity together such as hiking, rock climbing or rafting that requires them to work together to achieve goals.

At the end of the day, or at other appropriate points, a consultant helps members debrief the activities, focusing on what they have learned in the areas of teamwork, interpersonal relationships, trust, and leadership. The insights and trust developed by team members at the lab are expected to transfer back to the work setting.

MORE OD INTERVENTIONS (continued)

Role Analysis Technique

Sometimes working together we have conflicts over what role we are supposed to be performing on a particular team. This is an intervention usually used to help team members understand and clarify one another's roles. It has been applied in a number of situations, from clarifying roles of members of newly formed teams to helping improve the working relationships of teams that have been together for some time. The process typically goes something like this:

► **Role analysis**

The person in a role takes their best shot at listing on an easel the duties and responsibilities of that role. The rest of the team modifies or adds to the list until they have reached a consensus.

► **Role expectations of other team members**

The person next lists their expectations of what the other team members are supposed to be doing to help him/her to perform the role. They discuss this list, adding and modifying until they reach consensus.

► **Team members' expectations of the person's role**

Now the members of the team take a turn at listing what they expect of the person as it impacts their own performances. Again, they discuss this list and reach consensus.

► **Role profile**

The person takes the lists and writes up a summary of what has been agreed upon. This summary is called the role profile.

The same procedure should be carried out for every member of the team.

Quality Circles

Quality Circles are groups of people who meet usually once a week to discuss quality problems and issues. Quality circles identify specific ways to improve quality and set up plans to accomplish these ideas. In some cases, they have the authority to enact the plan themselves; in other cases, they have to take the plan to a steering committee that has the authority to approve the plan.

Usually when a quality circle is set up, it is done with a supervisor and some or all of his/her direct reporting members. The manager, if not the entire group, is given training in quality control concepts such as statistical process control, group dynamics, communication skills, and the like.

Self-Directed Teams

Self-Directed Teams are also known as self-managed and self-regulating teams. One recent study found that nearly half of the Fortune 500 companies are using some type of these teams. In each organization they may be referred to by a different name, but the purpose and function is relatively constant.

Self-directed teams are teams that basically take on the authority and responsibility of the work themselves. Usually, the direct supervisor is no longer needed. They now report to a manager that may be the key liaison for several such teams.

The teams have such complete responsibility for the entire product or service that they often set their own production, work, and vacation schedules. In some cases they have the authority to fire and hire. Usually team members are expected to know several jobs within the team in order to maximize the team's flexibility and increase ownership of the work.

Some teams are paid on the basis of group, rather than individual, performance. Individuals can typically get more pay as they master new skills and knowledge critical to the team's performance. As you might expect, there is a great deal of emphasis placed on training and maximizing the expertise of every team member.

MORE OD INTERVENTIONS (continued)

Training Games and Exercises

Training games and exercises are widely used in OD interventions. Today there are numerous books with hundreds of training exercises and games, many of which are microinterventions that can be used in a variety of OD projects. For example, there are exercise/game books on team building, managing change, unblocking the organization, problem solving, coaching, interpersonal skills, and self-directed teams. Each of these activities may be an appropriate way to intervene to help a team or an individual learn a valuable lesson or skill that is needed to improve performance.

Electronic Team Building

Electronic Team Building (ETB) is team building using high-tech. Up to 50 people are seated in a horseshoe format in a room. Each person at the meeting has a computer, and they are all networked together. The people at the meeting are not allowed to talk; they must type their comments into the computer. A software program quickly sorts the information and then displays the messages on a central screen.

Because the meeting has no verbal communication, it cuts down on side conversations and actually moves things along fairly effectively. Each statement is better thought out when it is typed, and there are virtually no emotionally charged face-to-face conflicts, as you might have in other team building situations.

One company that has used ETB with over 7,000 people claims it has brought people closer together and has leveled the playing field so that everyone can have an equal say on important issues. Some of the best ideas come from people who have been too shy or less capable of expressing themselves in face-to-face meetings. (We will probably hear of team building via the Internet in the near future.)

Organizational Transformation

Organizational Transformation is a fairly recent intervention. This intervention is usually used when there is a need for a major organization-wide change because of a threat to the survival of the organization; for instance, downsizing, a takeover or merger, or massive profit losses. In other words, the organization doesn't have time for many of the traditional OD interventions that are more proactive in nature.

In a time of revolutionary and abrupt change, abrupt interventions are used to get things back to a state of equilibrium as soon as possible. Usually, a key senior manager (like Lee Iacocca at Chrysler) steps up and takes control in a very directive manner, providing guidance to the ship in order to get it out of rough and dangerous water. This person provides the vision and energy to keep people focused and on track as a new state of equilibrium is achieved.

Total Quality Management (TQM)

TQM is a system-wide approach to improving quality. It uses a combination of processes to improve the overall quality of the organization, such as statistical processes, quality circles, and employee empowerment programs like self-directed work teams. We learned a lesson from the Japanese when they turned their product quality image totally around from "junk" to "jewels" in a few decades, becoming a strong global force to be reckoned with. Japan gave us a wake-up call, and TQM was the leading answer of the time.

Many of the traditional principles of OD are found in TQM, such as participative management emphasis, a lot of team building, top management support, and development of individual skills. In addition, TQM has introduced many new areas of emphasis, such as benchmarking, statistical measurements for quality control, emphasis on both internal and external customers, as well as the idea of continuous improvement.

MORE OD INTERVENTIONS (continued)

Learning Organizations

The Learning Organization is a fairly recent organization-wide intervention. The change agent here is attempting to develop a critical mass of individuals and groups who continuously learn. Through continuous learning, participants are always open to and searching for new paradigms and ways to do things more competitively.

The learning organization creates a culture that does the following:

- Removes barriers to learning

- Rewards failure if undertaken in a spirit of trial-and-error learning

- Encourages "new possibility" thinking and paradigm shifts

- Places a heavy emphasis on training and education

- Increases feedback mechanisms so that greater information flows into the system and, in turn, allows for greater output and the possibility of innovation

- Is humble enough to learn from everyone and every situation

- Is not satisfied to stay at any plateau and is constantly looking for the next growth cycle—in or out of its comfort zone

Search Conferences

The Search Conference is also a rather new intervention that has been derived from a combination of other interventions such as visioning, open systems, and future planning. Ideally, you gather the entire system in a conference setting for a meeting. The meeting may last two or three days. As many stakeholders as possible should be invited, including outside suppliers, stockholders, community leaders, etc. Care should be taken to invite those people who have vision, energy, and a proactive attitude toward growth and change.

Small groups are formed to work on these main events or activities:

1. They recall the past history of the organization in some detail, identifying significant trends. Then the small groups report back.

2. They then identify the most important trends of the present situation by finding newspaper and magazine articles to prove their points and act as a basis for discussion. Again, the small groups report back and the entire conference develops a list of top trends from all the group lists.

3. Then they repeat #2, this time focusing on the best and worst trends inside the organization.

4. The last event is to develop a picture of the "preferred future." This leads to a final list of priorities of the desired future organization by the entire conference.

MORE OD INTERVENTIONS (continued)

Performance Management

Performance Management is an intervention that has come about as result of OD consultants' work in setting up new structural systems. The goal is to align performance appraisal, goal-setting training, and reward systems with individual performance and business strategies. A fully integrated performance management system reinforces employee skills that produce the output the organization is looking for.

While this is not a new concept, it has only recently achieved a level of success—probably because in the past there was not a high enough level of employee ownership and participation to make it work. For this intervention to succeed employees have to believe they are not just being manipulated by management to work harder without any reward. With higher levels of empowerment and clear rewards linked to performance, this intervention can be highly effective.

Appreciative Inquiry

This is an newer intervention that focuses more on the positive strengths of the organization (what's good about it), rather than on the problems and what's wrong. A consultant begins by interviewing key individuals to find out what they think are the positives. This leads up to a meeting with as many attendees as possible from the organization to focus on what they appreciate about the organization.

The format is similar to the open systems planning and search conferences where the larger group is divided into smaller groups and they answer key questions such as these:

- What do you value and like about your work, co-workers, and the organization?

- What are the strengths of the department? The organization?

- When have you felt the department/organization most valued your contributions?

- When have you felt the most excitement and energy in your work here?

- What characteristics and qualities does this organization have that, if released, would be powerful and explosive?

- If we could put our money and time into magnifying one or two key strengths of you, the department, the entire organization . . . what would they be?

- If you could do anything you wanted to do to build the muscles of this organization, what would you do?

- What is the most satisfying thing this organization has ever done for its employees? Customers? Stockholders? The community?

Reengineering

Reengineering is an intervention that takes a look at every process within the business to see if systems can be redesigned to improve the performance of the organization. The intervention calls for new and unprecedented processes that improve performance by tearing down traditional structures and combining others to come up with new more efficient ways of doing things.

Some of the champions of reengineering take a more task-oriented approach, with little emphasis on the humanistic and social side of the ledger. Other experts of reengineering with an OD background have had excellent success with a balanced approach to reengineering. Combining both sides of the ledger can lead to powerful and significant results in organizational success.

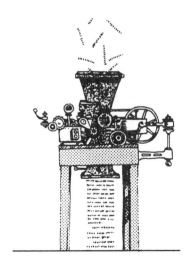

MORE OD INTERVENTIONS (continued)

Transorganizational Development

This an emerging OD intervention. As the world becomes smaller and yet more complex with the technical and information explosions, there is a greater need to build "win-win" alliances between organizations. Some key organizations have already gotten a headstart in this direction. However, it is uncharted ground for both the organizations and the consultants involved.

Thomas Cummings and Christopher Worley have worked in this area and have identified four stages of transorganizational development:

► **IDENTIFICATION STAGE**

Potential members are identified.

► **CONVENTION STAGE**

Potential members meet to assess the feasibility and mutual benefits of such an alliance.

► **ORGANIZATIONAL STAGE**

The members have decided to proceed; ground rules are set up defining the roles that will be served by the different members and how resources will be shared.

► **EVALUATION STAGE**

Processes are set up to measure and assess progress.

CASE STUDY PART 3

Results

After the retreat, the group should be feeling a sense of accomplishment because they have come together as a team. Working together with a change agent, they have come away from the retreat with specific plans on how to improve each of the issues that have been preventing them from functioning effectively as a team.

CASE STUDY PART 4

Follow-up

Dale knows that it is not over quite yet. It takes twenty-one days to establish a new habit or behavior. She will set up follow-up mechanisms, such as short meetings with the team, to assess progress and reward and encourage everyone involved to accomplish the desired new behavior changes.

SUMMARY

Whether you are new to OD or an experienced practitioner, this brief guide was designed to help you sort through the basic concepts of organization development.

If you have worked through the numerous checklists, steps, and exercises, begun to work through the diagnostic process and practiced with data collection methods, you will find that you can begin an immediate, successful implementation of OD.

Whether you decide to hire an OD consultant, do the work yourself, or some combination of the two, keep this book as a handy guide to consult time and again.

OD RESOURCES

Support Associations

Academy of Management
Division of Organization Development and Change
P.O. Box 3020
Briarcliff, NY 10510

American Society for Training and Development
OD Division
1640 King Street
Alexandria, VA 22313-2043

OD Institute
781 Beta Drive, Suite K
Cleveland, OH 44143

OD Network
76 South Orange Avenue, Suite 101
South Orange, NJ 07079

References

Burke, Warner W., Lawrence, P. Clark, and Cheryl Koopman. "Improve Your OD Project's Chances for Success." *Training and Development Journal.* September, 1984.

Cummings, Thomas G., and Cristopher G. Worley. *Organization Development and Change.* St. Paul, MN: West Publishing Company, 1993.

Eubanks, James L., Julie B. Marshal, and Michael P. O'Driscoll. "A Competency Model for OD Practitioners." *Training and Development Journal.* November, 1990.

Fordyce, Jack K., and Raymond Weil. *Managing with People.* Reading, MA: Addison-Wesley Publishing Co., 1971.

French, Wendell L. "An Action Research Model for Organization Development," *California Management Review.* Vol. XII, No. 2, 1969.

OD RESOURCES (continued)

MacEvoy, Bruce. "Change Leaders and the New Media." *American Demographics.* January, 1994.

McBer and Company Competency Model. "How to Get Top-Notch Change Agents." *Training and Development Journal.* December, 1993.

Nalder, David A. "A Comparison of Different Methods of Data Collection," *Feedback and Organization Development: Using Data-Based Methods.* Reading, MA: Addison-Wesley Publishing Co., 1977.

Shepard, Kenneth O., and Anthony P. Raia. "The OD Training Challenge," *Training and Development Journal.* April, 1981.

Smye, Marti and Robert Cooke. "The Key to Corporate Survival: Change Begins and Ends with People," In *The Change Management Handbook.* Edited by Lance Berger, et al. Burr Ridge, IL: Irwin, 1994.

Van Eynde, Donald F., Allan Church, Robert F. Hurley, and W. Warner Burke. "What OD Practitioners Believe," *Training & Development.* April. 1992.

Assessment

ORGANIZATION DEVELOPMENT

ORGANIZATION DEVELOPMENT
A PRACTITIONER'S TOOL KIT

A FIFTY-MINUTE™ BOOK

The objectives of this book are:

1. to define and explain Organization Development.

2. to provide models and methods for Organization Development.

3. to discuss the role of the Organization Development consultant or change agent.

4. to propose psychological strategies for managing change.

OBJECTIVE ASSESSMENT FOR ORGANIZATION DEVELOPMENT

Select the best response.

1. Organization Development (OD) is
   A. financial analysis.
   B. reducing errors.
   C. planned change.
   D. understanding the competition.

2. OD depends upon principles found in
   A. engineering.
   B. behavioral science.
   C. military science.
   D. physical science.

3. Collaboration is a key element in OD.
   A. True
   B. False

4. Employees contribute most to the success of an organization if
   A. they have many years of service.
   B. they are competent in following directions.
   C. they are empowered to be creative.

5. An OD consultant can be successful only if the
   A. organization has clear objectives.
   B. consultant has expertise.
   C. responsibilities of the organization are spelled out.
   D. all of the above

6. A survey revealed that OD practitioners value organizational
   A. processes more.
   B. outcomes more.

7. OD consultants encourage the tried and true.
   A. True
   B. False

8. It is usually best to use
   A. an external OD consultant.
   B. an internal OD consultant.
   C. both of the above as a team.

OBJECTIVE ASSESSMENT (continued)

9. Before any changes will take place, an organizational development consultant must
   A. have a good track record.
   B. have developed trust.
   C. be a specialist.

10. The Action Research model for OD requires data gathering and
    A. action throughout the process.
    B. then action when all data has been collected.

11. In general, Force Field Analysis evaluates the strengths and weaknesses of
    A. forces that maintain the status quo.
    B. forces for change.
    C. driving and restraining forces.

12. Good OD practice requires that
    A. employee questionnaires be used.
    B. actual behavior be observed.
    C. employee interviews be held.
    D. survey feedback be provided.

13. Change management requires that
    A. resistance be minimal.
    B. a vision be supported.
    C. old ways be accepted.
    D. continued competence be assumed.

14. Most change management fails because of poor strategy.
    A. True
    B. False

15. People tend to resist change because
    A. it is too much effort.
    B. they fear loss.
    C. they don't like to learn.

16. A change agent
    A. must be part of management.
    B. should be a hired consultant.
    C. can be any inspired individual.
    D. should be appointed.

17. When you have no control over change, your best recourse is to
    A. be reactive and resistant.
    B. protect your interests.
    C. choose a positive approach.
    D. any of the above

18. A change agent should be able to
    A. relate well to people.
    B. collect data and accurately analyze it.
    C. persuade and influence.
    D. design training.
    E. all of the above

19. A useful intervention technique for OD consultants is to ask conflicting individuals to
    A. give up their differences.
    B. write down their differences.
    C. generalize about each other's behavior.
    D. allow the consultant to decide solutions.

20. An OD laboratory group
    A. solves problems.
    B. should have required participation.
    C. helps people understand behavior.
    D. all of the above

21. In process consultation, an OD consultant
    A. listens, questions, clarifies and synthesizes.
    B. observes processes.
    C. helps people solve their own problems.
    D. all of the above

22. The function of an "organizational mirror" is for a group to observe another group's processes and then to
    A. keep their conclusions to themselves.
    B. share what they have observed with the other group.
    C. show the other group how to change.

23. An attitude survey
    A. usually gets everyone involved.
    B. can be a measurement tool.
    C. may not work if management lacks implementation skills.
    D. all of the above

OBJECTIVE ASSESSMENT (continued)

24. An advantage of electronic team building is that everyone can have an equal say.
    A. True
    B. False

25. Reengineering should
    A. emphasize a task-oriented approach.
    B. change traditional structures.
    C. include humanistic considerations.
    D. all of the above

Qualitative Objectives for *Organization Development*

To define and explain Organization Development

   Questions 1, 2, 3, 12

To provide models and methods for Organization Development

   Questions 10, 11, 19, 20, 21, 22, 23, 24, 25

To discuss the role of the Organization Development consultant or change agent

   Questions 5, 6, 7, 8, 9, 16, 18

To propose psychological strategies for managing change

   Questions 4, 13, 14, 15, 17

ANSWER KEY

1. C	**10.** A	**18.** E
2. B	**11.** C	**19.** B
3. A	**12.** D	**20.** C
4. C	**13.** B	**21.** D
5. D	**14.** B	**22.** B
6. A	**15.** B	**23.** D
7. B	**16.** C	**24.** A
8. C	**17.** C	**25.** C
9. B		

Copyright © 1996, Crisp Publications, Inc.
1200 Hamilton Court
Menlo Park, California 94025

NOTES

NOTES

NOTES

NOTES

NOTES

NOW AVAILABLE FROM
CRISP PUBLICATIONS

Books • Videos • CD Roms • Computer-Based Training Products

If you enjoyed this book, we have great news for you. There are over 200 books available in the *50-Minute*™ Series. To request a free full-line catalog, contact your local distributor or Crisp Publications, Inc., 1200 Hamilton Court, Menlo Park, CA 94025. Our toll-free number is 800-422-7477.

Subject Areas Include:

Management

Human Resources

Communication Skills

Personal Development

Marketing/Sales

Organizational Development

Customer Service/Quality

Computer Skills

Small Business and Entrepreneurship

Adult Literacy and Learning

Life Planning and Retirement

CRISP WORLDWIDE DISTRIBUTION

English language books are distributed worldwide. Major international distributors include:

ASIA/PACIFIC

Australia/New Zealand: In Learning, PO Box 1051 Springwood QLD, Brisbane, Australia 4127
Telephone: 7-3841-1061, Facsimile: 7-3841-1580   ATTN: Messrs. Gordon

Singapore: Graham Brash (Pvt) Ltd. 32, Gul Drive, Singapore 2262
Telephone: 65-861-1336, Facsimile: 65-861-4815   ATTN: Mr. Campbell

CANADA

Reid Publishing, Ltd., Box 69559-109 Thomas Street, Oakville,
Ontario Canada L6J 7R4.
Telephone: (905) 842-4428, Facsimile: (905) 842-9327   ATTN: Mr. Reid

Trade Book Stores: Raincoast Books, 8680 Cambie Street,
Vancouver, British Columbia, Canada V6P 6M9.
Telephone: (604) 323–7100, Facsimile: 604-323-2600   ATTN: Ms. Laidley

EUROPEAN UNION

England: Flex Training, Ltd. 9-15 Hitchin Street, Baldock,
Hertfordshire, SG7 6A, England
Telephone: 1-462-896000, Facsimile: 1-462-892417   ATTN: Mr. Willetts

INDIA

Multi-Media HRD, Pvt., Ltd., National House, Tulloch Road, Appolo Bunder,
Bombay, India 400-039
Telephone: 91-22-204-2281, Facsimile: 91-22-283-6478   ATTN: Messrs. Aggarwal

MIDDLE EAST

United Arab Emirates: Al-Mutanabbi Bookshop, PO Box 71946, Abu Dhabi
Telephone: 971-2-321-519, Facsimile: 971-2-317-706   ATTN: Mr. Salabbai

SOUTH AMERICA

Mexico: Grupo Editorial Iberoamerica, Serapio Rendon #125, Col. San Rafael,
06470 Mexico, D.F.
Telephone: 525-705-0585, Facsimile: 525-535-2009   ATTN: Señor Grepe

SOUTH AFRICA

Alternative Books, Unit A3 Sanlam Micro Industrial Park, Hammer Avenue
STRYDOM Park, Randburg, 2194 South Africa
Telephone: 2711 792 7730, Facsimile: 2711 792 7787   ATTN: Mr. de Haas